HANDS THAT HEAL

HANDS THAT HEAL

by Echo Bodine Burns

International Standard Book Number 0-917086-76-7

Cover Design by Matt Barna

Illustrations by Richard Mansir

Living/Living Dead Illustration
with permission of Inner Creations, Inc., Chicago, Ill.

Poem with permission of Elizabeth Searle Lamb

Printed in the United States of America

Published by ACS Publications, Inc.
P.O. Box 16430
San Diego, CA 92116-0430

First Printing, February 1986
Second Printing, January 1987

Dedication

I would like to dedicate this book to Joan L. Harrington.

Also by ACS Publications, Inc.

Contents

Acknowledgments

Writing this book has been a process for me. Many wonderful people helped me through this process and I would like to acknowledge and sincerely thank them.

Alberto Aquas — through your example, I finally gave myself permission to be me.

Mary Anderson — for all the hours and hard work you put into editing, typing and generally putting this book into order. I couldn't have done it without you.

Lynne Burmyn — the book would still be sitting on my desk if you hadn't taken the initiative and sent it to the publisher! Thank you for all your encouragement.

My parents, Ed and Mae; my brothers Scott and Michael; and my sister, Nikki — thank you for helping me accept and understand my gifts over the last nineteen years.

My husband, Jim — for patiently going through this process with me, for being my sounding board, for pushing me when I needed a push, for believing in me when I couldn't. (Wouldn't!)

To all my wonderful friends — who have been so encouraging and supportive for many years.

To the hundreds of clients I have worked with over the years — through you I learned about spiritual healing.

To William Kittleson — who took time from a busy Sunday afternoon's schedule to take pictures of me for this book.

To Maritha Pottenger — for your loving and encouraging letters. Your enthusiasm gave me the final push to help make this book become **a book.**

Thank you to all of you. You have each played such an important part in this process.

* * *

The stories in this book are true accounts, but the names of the individuals involved have been changed.

Healing Hands

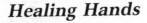
by Elizabeth Searle Lamb

Dear God, let my hands
be always hands of healing
through which Your life
may radiate to lessen pain,
to bring a renewal of peace
and healing wherever needed.

Dear God, let my hands
bring through their touch
some essence of Your love
flowing through them
to bring comfort and joy.
I offer my hands as a channel;
use them as Your healing tools.

Introduction

When I was seventeen years old, I went to a medium for a psychic reading. She told me I was born with the gift of healing and that God would use me as a channel for His* healing energy.

You may be thinking: "Oh, you lucky girl, how wonderful!" Well, to be truthful, I was pretty upset. I instantly pictured myself running around the country, wearing white robes and being very religious, and never again having any fun. Just healing sick people, and praying a lot.

I was so confused! I didn't know what to think or what to do. The only healers I had ever heard of were Jesus Christ and Oral Roberts. I felt an overwhelming sense of responsibility that I didn't particularly want.

The medium told me to go home to my father, who was in bed with a migraine headache. She told me to lay my hands on his head. She said God would use my hands as instruments to channel His healing energy to my father.

---

* For the sake of uniformity, the author has in this book, used the pronouns "He" and "It" or "Himself" and "Itself" interchangeably when referring to God, realizing that in the spiritual literature of the world the varying concepts of God have been given many different names.

I remember being so excited, but at the same time feeling like some kind of freak. What would my friends say? But I also fantasized about traveling all over the world healing every sick person I could find. I remember thinking, "I must be special." And the very next thought that followed was, "Why me? I haven't done anything special to deserve this."

All of those conflicting thoughts and feelings took place within a thirty-minute drive home that night. Part of me felt grand. Another part felt scared. Another, very responsible, and another, completely in the dark about what to do or how to do it. I wanted God to talk to me about what it all meant.

When I arrived home I told my father what the medium had said. I asked him if I could put my hands on his head. Within a minute, my hands became very hot. I could actually sense an energy inside. It was slight, and I was sure I was imagining the whole thing. I kept my hands on his head for probably five minutes at the most. (It seemed like five hours!) My hands cooled down to their normal temperature, and it felt like the energy had stopped. I looked at my father, expecting him to tell me I was crazy. But instead, he said his headache was gone.

I'm not going to elaborate further on how I felt. But I will share with you the fact that for days, possibly weeks, after that experience I continued to have all the same thoughts, feelings, fears and questions I had that night on my way home from the medium's.

Now, seventeen more years have passed in my life since that first laying-on-hands healing took place, and I have learned several things through trial and error that I want to pass on to you.

I would like to stress right here in big, bold letters that **I am not an authority** on this subject. My reason for writing this book is to pass on the bits and pieces of knowledge I have gathered along the way about heal-ing in order to help you work with your channeling gift.

One of the continuing frustrations I run into with this gift is that there is very little written about laying-on-hands healing. There are books written about healers, but I have yet to find a book written by healers, and I have yet to find a book that has shown me what to do and what not to do in a simple, straightforward way.

I believe God heals. I believe that all of us have the potential to be channels for God's healing energy. I have felt the energy. I have seen the results. There is nothing complicated about God's healing energy.

> **There is nothing complicated about God's healing energy. Anyone can be a channel for God's healing energy.**

Chapter 1

The Healing Energy

Have you ever noticed your hands becoming unusually warm, or that they feel "full"? Almost as if there's something in them? What I'm describing is **healing energy**. The sensation is **hard** to put into words and even **harder** to explain. Very simply put, though, Jesus Christ told us we all have the power within ourselves to heal the sick.

I believe this healing energy comes from the God within each one of us.

The energy is not always hot. Sometimes the full feeling is so intense, my hands and arms shake or jerk. Sometimes during a healing my whole upper body feels like it's trembling. My clients each have different ways of experiencing the energy. Some say it feels like bolts of energy flowing through their body. Others say the energy feels like a cool mentholatum going into their body. Some have asked me to take my hands off their bodies because the heat is too intense. Some talk about seeing themselves surrounded in a white light during the healing. Others say they feel pain. Some say they feel nothing. Each client is different. My experience with each client is different, too. No two healings have ever been alike.

The biggest reason this book has taken me so long to write is that I've thought in order to get a book published, it needs to be a big one, full of pages and full of explanations. Coming up with lots of pages full of explanations is difficult to do when the topic is spiritual healing because the truth is very simple.

> God heals people. God's
> healing energy flows through us
> to heal physical and emotional
> problems.

A Healing Session

I would like to share with you, step by step, the process I go through with each individual who comes for a healing.

The first time a person comes for a healing, they are usually somewhat apprehensive about the experience, so I invite them to sit down and talk to me about their reason for needing the healing. I explain to them that I am not the healer — that I am a channel for God's healing energy. I tell them my hands may become warm and may tremble, and that it's simply the healing energy.

I tell them I do not know how many healings they will need. Each person is unique in their healing process. I tell them that I am also clairvoyant and if I see any images of their physical condition, I will share the information with them when the healing is done.

They may have some old, blocked emotions which may be unblocked by the healing energy, and they may want to cry during the healing, which is why I have a box of tissues right on the healing table.

I encourage them to flow with their body. I tell them that whatever they need to do is okay with me. If they need to cry, or feel like laughing, or fall asleep, or would feel more comfortable talking — that's fine. I tell them the healing takes twenty minutes, and ask that they remain lying down for at least five to ten minutes after I am done.

I have found that if some people get up as soon as I am done channeling the energy, they feel light-headed. Some are disoriented. I tell everyone to please remain lying down for at least five to ten minutes, or until they feel they have "come back." Coming back means feeling connected to themselves, feeling a sense of where they are, feeling awake and clear-headed. Some clients sleep up to an hour after the healing, which I believe is very beneficial to the healing process.

I tell them it's not necessary to remove any clothing for the healing. I ask them if they are comfortable being touched. If they are not comfortable with it, I keep my hands one or two inches above their body during the healing. I ask them if they are ready to begin. If they're ready, I ask them to lie down on my healing table. If you don't have a healing table, a bed or couch works just as well. But remember — you are going to be sitting or standing for twenty minutes, maybe longer, so you need to be comfortable, too. If they are cold, I cover them with a blanket.

As they are lying down and getting situated, I go and wash my hands. I wash my hands for a couple of

reasons. One, because I do not want any kind of odor on my hands which might offend my client. The other reason is that it is a way for me to center myself. While washing, I focus my attention on being a channel for healing. It's a "getting ready" ritual for me. Then I close the drapes in my office and turn on a twenty minute tape of relaxing music. I use Steve Halpern or Golden Voyage tapes. There are several wonderful tapes on the market.

I place a white handkerchief where I am going to place my hands. This is because sometimes my hands get hot and they sweat, so it's mainly for the comfort of the client.

Silently, I say the Prayer of Protection (Chapter Five), and thank God for using me as a channel for His healing energy, and for directing me with the healing. I sit beside my healing table with my hands at a comfortable level and place my hands on the troubled area. Within a couple of minutes I feel the flow of energy. My hands begin to warm up. I usually remain silent, listening to my inner voice for direction. Sometimes I will get a strong intuitive feeling to move my hands; other times my hands remain where they are.

For years, the energy flowed only through my right hand, but about six years ago it began flowing out of my left hand, too. What I prefer to do is put one hand on the troubled area and the other on my client's solar plexus.

I have heard the solar plexus referred to as the "battery" of the body. It is a great network of nerves situated in the upper part of the abdomen. I visualize those nerves carrying healing energy to every part of the body.

I continue to listen to my inner voice for any direction I may need, or that my client may need. When the twenty-minute tape is done, I remove my hands.

5

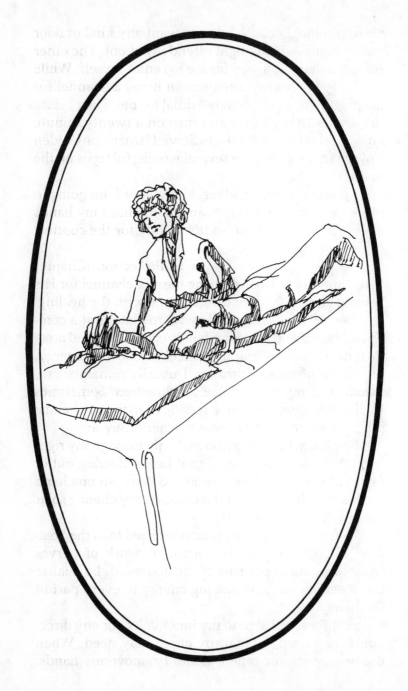

On some occasions, my hands feel "stuck" to the person, so I just let the energy flow until my hands feel free to move. Then I tell the individual to lie there as long as they would like, and I leave the room.

I usually shake my hands several times after a healing and wash them. I shake them to release any energy left in my hands. Sometimes my hands feel "full" of energy after a healing, almost to the point of an aching kind of feeling, so I shake the energy out. Then I wash them, if they are still hot, to cool them down.

After the client is up, I ask them what the healing was like for them. I ask them if they have any questions. Sometimes a person will feel more pain initially after a healing. Even though I'm not sure this is the correct answer (and I tell them that), I say that I believe the healing brought the pain more to the surface and that it will only be temporary. Every client so far who did experience more pain initially has told me it was usually gone within five to thirty minutes after leaving.

You may want to share with a client who has come with a head cold, bronchitis, emphysema or asthma, that they may cough or sneeze a lot after the healing. The healing will loosen everything up for that is the body's way of getting rid of the infection.

We then set up another appointment if the client wants to continue the process. I always make sure they are fully awake when they leave. Some feel very energized after a session, some are very relaxed. I always allow enough time between clients in case they have a need to talk.

When a person calls for a healing, I mark out one hour in my appointment book. Five minutes is to discuss their healing need. Twenty to thirty minutes are for the healing. The time remaining is for them to wake up at their own pace without feeling rushed and for them to share what the healing was like for them.

They may have physical sensations, emotional feelings or mental images like "seeing" their body heal. There have been times when I have had to wake a client. I always wake them very gently. The healing energy is very calming and I don't want to do anything to disrupt that serenity such as loudly waking them and telling them they "have to leave right now."

Many people ask me what happens to me during a healing session. I feel the energy. I relax. I pray. I listen. I always feel very good after channeling a healing.

Absentee Healings

Absentee healings are healings that take place when you, the channel, are not in the presence of the person receiving the healing. Here's what I do when I'm sending an absentee healing.

I sit down. I center on the person who has asked for the healing. I visualize the healing taking place as if they were right in front of me. I ask God to please heal so-and-so. I wait until I feel a "connection" with the person. It's an intuitive feeling. Then I say "Thank you," knowing that the healing is taking place, and I either go on to the next person on my list or go on about my day. My part takes between two to five minutes, depending upon how long it takes for me to feel the connection.

Absentee healing does work. Whenever someone calls with a healing need and you are not able to get to them for a few days, tell them you can send absentee healings. Ask when they would be able to sit down for a while and receive the healing. I'm a night owl, so I usually channel healing late at night when the client is in bed. Many times I pray for absentee healing twice a day for someone. You'll have to decide what's best

for you and what fits in with your schedule.

You should tell the client they may experience the warmth or tingles of the healing energy. I've had many clients report back to me that they felt the heat or the tingling. Some have said they could feel the hands on their body.

I have received numerous calls and letters from clients over the years letting me know they began to experience the healing energy immediately after calling and making a request for absentee healing. As I have said earlier, the healing energy is universal. The process begins as soon as a person asks — which in dicates they have opened themselves up to the healing energy. You might be wondering, "Couldn't I just pray for absentee healing for everyone that calls?" Yes, you could.

Anyone can send healing
energy to another being at
any time.

Chapter 2

Not Everyone Is Ready to Be Healed

Hard to believe? I know. It was hard for me to believe that everyone who is sick is not ready to be healed, just like that. But if you're going to be a channel for healing, you need to accept that some don't want healing. The fact is: we can't interfere in other people's lives. Just because we may believe they would be happier or better off if they were healed doesn't make it true.

Remember in the *Bible* that Jesus asked people if they wanted to be healed? I used to think that was kind of a dumb question, but I no longer do. It's a simple question, but the reasons for it are very important, and not always so simple.

There are several reasons people get sick, and while I'm certainly not an authority on the whys of illness, I will pass on to you some of the things I have come to understand. Some of the reasons discussed here may be operating as unconscious motivators more than as conscious choices. But they are important.

12

Which Am I?

Love

Helpfulness	Ability
Forgiveness	Humility
Generosity	Power
Patience	Peace
Gratitude	Selflessness
Trust	**Faith**
Joy	Abundance
Freedom	Brotherhood
Praise	Truth
Strength	Health
Success	Good will

Living?

Service

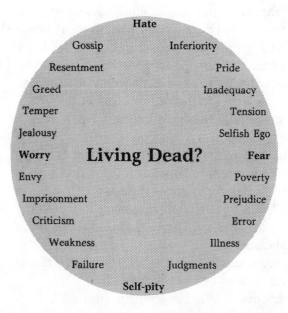

Hate

Gossip	Inferiority
Resentment	Pride
Greed	Inadequacy
Temper	Tension
Jealousy	Selfish Ego
Worry	**Fear**
Envy	Poverty
Imprisonment	Prejudice
Criticism	Error
Weakness	Illness
Failure	Judgments

Living Dead?

Self-pity

From concept by Martha Pottenger

"Reasons" for Illness

1. Our culture has in the last few years gotten much better about allowing us to take "mental health" days off work, but there are still some of us who believe we have to do an "honest" day's work, five days a week, no matter what. The only excuse for not doing what we perceive as "our share" is to be sick. So, we get sick! We get a day or two off. We get well, and go back to work.

2. I have met children who have learned that the only way to get the nurturing and tenderness they need is by being sick. I have also met several adults like that.

3. There are people who are learning some valuable lessons through their illness, important for their spiritual development.
I believe that sixty percent of all illness starts with an emotion that is trapped within the body. It could be hurt feelings, anger, fear, resentment. It could be lack of forgiveness of ourself or of others. It could be self-hatred, or wanting to punish yourself or someone else. Some people react to the unfairness in life by sub-consciously creating illness. When I have a health challenge myself, the first thing I do is talk to my emotions. I ask my body what it is that the illness is trying to tell me. Am I holding in some emotions that I need to express? If I'm willing to know the answer, it always will come. If I don't get a clear message, I look at the specific body-part that is in pain. I think about what it might symbolize.
Here are some examples of what I'm talking about when I say an illness can symbolize something.
Eye Problems — What is going on in my life I am not seeing clearly, or don't want to look at?

Ear Problems — What's being said to me that I don't want to hear?

Throat Problems — Is there something I want to say to someone that I am holding back? Do I find something in my life "hard to swallow?"

Get the idea? I keep it as simple as possible. I don't believe it's always as simple as some of the above examples, though. They are meant only to indicate that illness has its own kind of meaning or language much of the time, and knowing that can help us in our healing of ourselves and of our clients.

Here is a little method that can sometimes be helpful in trying to understand a particular problem: I always get this little picture in my head when I'm dealing with physical problems.

The solar plexus seems to be our emotional center. When we "stuff" emotions, either by denying them or minimizing them, they stay "stuck." Our feelings do what they can to be released, but when we're not cooperating with that releasing process, the emotions start working away at the physical body. Sometimes they are stored up for years, but usually the physical aches and pains come shortly after emotional pains have occurred which were not expressed.

I've come to see how deadly stored anger can be. Many people I have seen have stored resentments since childhood. Fear is another devastating emotion. Three years ago I had surgery to correct blockages in my colon. Through hypnosis I saw my colon was filled with fears. I think because most of my life I have felt awkward about expressing emotion, I have stored most of them up and have learned first-hand how devastating their effects on the body can be. Needless to say, and awkward or not, I am learning to express my emotions!

4. I have met people with physical problems that

15

do not feel worthy of being healed. They believe sickness is a punishment they deserve from God.

5. There are those who have been sick for so long or who have grown so dependent on illness to get them what they want, that the thought of functioning in a healthy body and learning the new life style it would require is too threatening.

6. Another area to consider when working with illness is *karma*. Each of us is a unique child of God. Each of us has our own path to follow in this lifetime, and depending upon what we've been up to in our past lives, there are certain experiences we may need to have in order to learn and grow spiritually the way we need to.

Always remember: don't force your will on anyone!

Don't assume that anyone with a physical problem is ready for, wants, or should have a healing.

It is very important to the healing process that the person suffering **ask** for the healing, themselves. You can certainly let the person know you channel healing energy, but leave it up to them to ask for it.

Another important thing to remember:

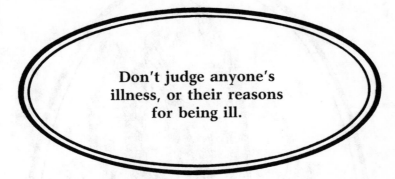

**Don't judge anyone's
illness, or their reasons
for being ill.**

We human beings want to know the "whys" of everything. Many people on a "spiritual path" judge illness as "failure." They feel any physical problems are signs of emotional/mental/spiritual dis-ease. Such a judgmental attitude can be very hard on other people — and on the individual himself when he becomes sick! Feelings of guilt or inadequacy just impede the healing process. We need to love ourselves enough to be open to God's love healing us.

If life is truly a learning experience and we come here to experience, to master life, to expand our boundaries then perhaps some people are experiencing physical handicaps or illness as an ultimate "challenge" to overcome. Or, perhaps a physical ailment presents an individual with the opportunity to more easily go inward and concentrate on other sides of life. Or, an illness may assist the person in developing empathy, patience or a number of other attributes. It is not our job to judge — either ourselves or another party. We are responsible only for ourselves and can choose healing if we wish.

Chapter 3

How Long Does It Take to Be Healed?

Almost every time I start channeling energy to someone, they want to know how many visits it will take before they are healed. Since Jesus Christ was the only Healer I ever read about and all of His healings appeared to be instantaneous, I wondered why it was that some people didn't get healed instantly when I channeled healing energy to them. For a long time I feared I lacked something. I would think that maybe I should pray more, or attend church more than once a week. I did both, and it didn't make any difference.

**People get healed when
they are ready to be healed!**

Before you start doing healings on a new person, explain to them you do not know how many sessions they will need. They may have to come back several times, or they may be healed after the first session. Some people believe that healing is hard work and therefore takes time and effort. Some believe the more serious the ailment, the more time it should take to heal. Some people are working on liking themselves well enough to allow the healing and it takes time for them to achieve sufficient self-appreciation. Some have "secondary gains" from being ill (such as gaining attention, getting out of doing something they dislike, getting disability, etc.) and resist healing (perhaps unconsciously) until ready to give up their payoffs. Healing is a change — and many people resist changing (even when it seems to their betterment); change seems frightening. Even the security of illness may appeal more. The "reasons" for differences in the time people take to heal are many. The fact is that we cannot predict how long any given individual will require for healing.

There is another side to all of this. There are the clients who feel their illness is the healer's problem. Doctors certainly must deal with this same thing, all the time. My doctor always tells me to take all the medication until it's gone, and not to stop halfway through because I feel better. Not being a doctor, I can't say anything to my clients. This is because I don't know how many sessions they are going to need, or what exactly their healing process is going to entail. I just have to hope that the clients care enough about themselves to continue receiving healing until they feel truly healed.

In almost every healing I have channeled, a process seems to take place within the person. If you are going to use your channeling gift, **you need to be**

22

patient with the process. The process is unique for each person. Clients may connect with themselves in a deeper way. They may release old emotions, old blocks, old memories — memories from past lives, or memories from this lifetime. They may work on forgiveness, self-doubt, self-hate, self-love, resentment, anger, letting go. Yet, they may experience "nothing" — just physical healing. This process is so individualized, no two healings are alike.

Stay as emotionally detached as you can. Don't get in there and try to hurry up the process. As I said earlier, we are each on our own path, going at our own pace, for a reason.

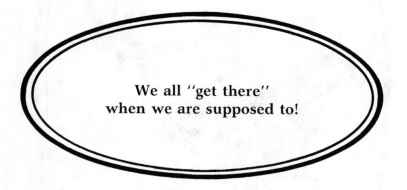

We all "get there"
when we are supposed to!

Chapter 4

You Have Your Own Inner Helper

I believe we are spiritual beings first, human beings second. We have all that we need right within us. God lives within each one of us. I believe our intuition is God speaking to us, guiding us on our path. I believe in order to be a channel for God's healing energy, it is very important for us to recognize and trust our intuition.

How good are you at trusting your intuition? Do you listen to that still, small voice within? Are you wondering what I'm talking about? How about "gut reaction," that sense or feeling inside yourself that directs you daily? Do you see images, get visual impressions of what to do? Are you a friend to that part of yourself or do you minimize your inner feelings, believing them to be not "real" enough to trust?

If you are one of those people who denies or minimizes your intuition, I strongly suggest you start paying attention to that part of yourself. I believe that God directs me each time I'm channeling His

wonderful healing energy, but it's up to me to pay attention!

The inner voice (or vision or feeling) may say, "Move your hands here; put your right hand over there; say this to the person; ask them this; stop the channeling; continue the channeling; have them (the client) come back twice this week — five times this week — once every two weeks." All that helpful guidance comes from God . . . if we listen, it's there! Let me also add that you may hear nothing or feel nothing or see nothing. That's okay, too. When it's time to know something, you will hear it, know it or feel it. **Be patient**!

So much of this channeling of healing energy is simply letting go and allowing the process to flow.

Chapter 5

Where Does the Illness Go?

I've been asked several times, "Do you ever get the person's illness?"

No, I have never picked
up a person's illness or gotten
physically sick myself from
channeling healing energy.

There have been times when I have felt a strange kind of pain in my hands while I'm channeling a healing, but it disappears immediately.

Before I begin a healing, I say the **Prayer of Protection** and visualize myself and the client surrounded in the White Light of Christ.

PRAYER OF PROTECTION

The Light of God surrounds me.
The Love of God enfolds me.
The Power of God protects me.
The Presence of God watches over me.
Wherever I am, God is!

As far as where the illness goes, I don't know the "real" answer. I have always assumed the disease is dissolved by the healing energy.

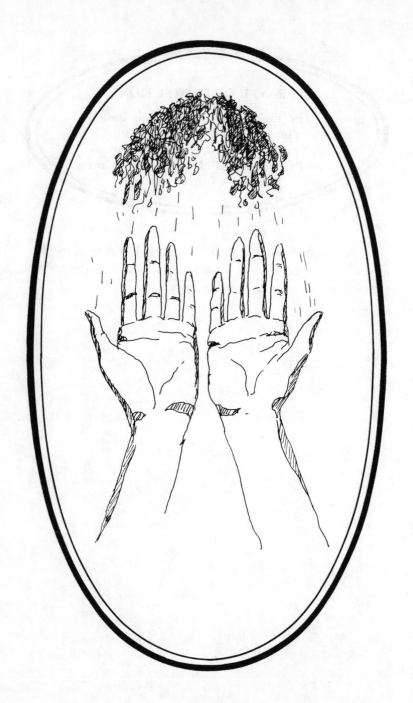

Chapter 6

Watch That Ego

ℋere is another short, but very important, chapter. It's about **ego**.

One of the things I have to always remind myself and my clients of is that I am not the Healer. God is the Healer. The energy that flows through us as channels is God's healing energy, not ours.

My ego feels wonderful when I hear someone say, "Echo healed me." I feel important. I feel needed. But I have found that I can't allow myself the luxury of feeling things like that. I need to always remember who the Healer is, and who the channel is. The day I start to believe that I am the one with the power, I'm in big trouble!!!

Let me explain what I mean by "big trouble." Being on the spiritual path I choose, I believe God is my source for **everything**! I ask God's guidance in all my affairs, whether it is work, my home, the finances, my relationships, my health or my shortcomings.

I lived a fair number of years without a close, trusting relationship with God. My life was pure

World's
Greatest
Healer

self-will — running riot. The difference between believing I was running the show, and relying on God for His inner guidance, is **incomparable**.

Before getting on a "spiritual path," I was a practicing alcoholic. I believed I ran the show. I was full of self-doubt. I had a lot of self-destructive behavior. I was too proud to reach out for help or admit to myself that I needed help. I made decisions about my life based on fear, anger, loneliness, resentments and low self-worth.

I had a false sense of ego in the sense of not wanting anyone to know who or what I really was, so I would project an image to people as someone who really had her life in order. I tried to project confidence and happiness, yet the whole time I was terrified because I felt so alone, so unhappy.

I tried controlling outcomes. I felt responsible for other people's happiness. I wasn't doing a very good job of taking care of myself, so I tried taking care of everyone else's life. I felt I knew what other people needed (self-will), and I would do whatever I could to get it for them, or to make them change. Before I came to believe in a Higher Power, I didn't know what a "flow" was.

After I joined a recovery program for alcoholics, I began to develop a personal relationship with my Higher Power. The program taught me God would restore me and my life, if I gave Him a chance. Over the years, I have come to rely on this power greater than myself to guide me in my daily life with all my affairs. Living without Divine Guidance is going backward for me. It's empty. It's scarey. Living with full acceptance of God is beautiful. It's flowing. It's harmonious.

So, when I say I'm in big trouble when I start believing I am the one with the power, I don't mean

33

I'm in trouble with God, or with my family, or with the law. I am in big trouble with myself in the sense that I am where I don't want to be!

God is the Healer!

Chapter 7

First Things First

I would like to share with you a phase I went through in channeling healings, with the hope that you can avoid it.

It was about seven years ago. I was a barber, working a full-time job during the day. When there was a need, I would channel healings in the evening. I never advertised myself as a spiritual healer, but the word was spreading fast. I was getting a lot of calls from people with physical problems.

At that point, I hadn't established any boundaries for myself. I felt such a sense of responsibility to anyone who needed a healing.

My life was getting way out of balance. During the day, I cut hair. At night, I would drive to different people's homes and channel healings.

Mentally I was feeling scattered. Physically, I was getting run down. I would drink a lot of caffeine and eat a lot of sugar to keep up with this pace.

I assumed that because I had this gift, this was how I was to live my life. I had no social life. No play time. No routine for myself.

I was getting to the point where I was feeling resentful about my gift. It felt more like a burden. That sense of responsibility I felt on the inside was driving me crazy! I was feeling resentful, which then I'd feel guilty about.

I don't remember how long this went on, but I do remember clearly what stopped all of it. I went through a three-day period of being very sick, followed by a two-week stay in the hospital which included surgery on my colon. Physically, I was completely run down. Mentally and emotionally, I was so confused. I was angry with God.

I had this idea in my head that as long as I was doing God's work, He would take care of me, so why was I in the hospital?

Clients were calling me at the hospital. Some were very upset with me. How could I be sick?" they'd ask. I was a healer. I wasn't supposed to get sick. They had forgotten I was a human being — but more importantly, I had forgotten.

It hadn't occurred to me that the first responsibility I had was to myself. I had no boundaries. I would say "yes" to everyone that called.

It wasn't God's fault that I was in the hospital. It turned out to be a blessing in disguise, because I was forced to stop that way of life **I had created** and take a look.

I was never very good at being assertive and saying "no." Setting boundaries for myself was very scarey and yet I knew it was essential for my health and well-being that I do so. I had to **learn** about a balanced way of life. Work, eating properly, getting eight hours of sleep every night, finding time to play, to be creative, to have a social life, to be alone, to keep up with my financial responsibilities, and staying on a spiritual path so that I was getting spiritually filled up — all these things needed a place in my life. In neglecting to keep these things balanced, I had overlooked a tremendous responsibility to myself . . . and I had to get back on the track.

Making Room for What's Important

I had a friend make a healing table for me, and I began to have my clients come to me for their healings instead of driving all over to do them.

I wish you could have seen my first healing table. It was great! It was made with an old metal ladder, some plywood, and some foam rubber. It was very comfortable. I was so proud of it. My friend made it high enough off the floor so that I could either sit or stand comfortably for as long as I needed. I sit during most of the healings that I channel, so it's important to have the table at a comfortable height for my arms.

At first I worried about asking the clients to come to my home, but no one objected. If a person cannot get here, I will go to them, but very seldom is that the case. Now I have a portable healing table that I can take with me if necessary. It is important when you are channeling energy that **you're** comfortable, too. It's hard on your neck and back and legs when you have to crouch down for long periods of time.

Next, I had to set up a consistent schedule for the nights I would do healings and the nights I was free to do what I needed to do to keep some balance and order in my life. The difficult part was sticking to the schedule saying to a client who had an urgent healing need that I had plans. That sense of responsibility inside

would stab me with guilt pangs.

If someone calls now, I make an appointment to see them and then send an absentee healing in the meantime.

One very important thing for you and your clients to remember is that you are only human. You are the channel. Your client can ask God for a healing, and you do not need to be present in order for the healing to work.

I had to develop a certain "detachedness" about illness. We are surrounded by human beings with physical problems. We can tell people we channel healing energy but leave the responsibility of getting the healing up to them.

Find Your Own "Rules"

I don't feel comfortable saying to you, "Do this," or "Don't do that." It is important for you to find what's right for **you**. What works for you.

I **do** feel comfortable asking you to be aware of the responsibility you have to yourself, however. Give some thought to boundaries. Be okay with your limitations. Give yourself permission to do what is right for you.

You are a channel for
healing. You are a child of God.
The better you take care of you — the better
you'll be able to channel that beautiful,
loving, healing energy.

Chapter 8

Questions Commonly Asked

People are fascinated by spiritual healing and always have a lot of questions. This chapter will cover the questions most commonly asked. I will also share with you the answers I have found to be true for myself. I would strongly suggest that you look within yourself for your own answers, for you will find that you have your own individual responses that may differ in some respects from my responses. But my own answers may help you in finding your own, for when people find out you're a channel for healing energy, you will be asked a lot of these same questions.

Question: Are you drained after a healing?

Answer: Never. It's not my energy that I channel.

Question: Is there any physical problem that can't be healed?

40

Answer: This question always strikes me funny. The answer is **no**. I have never come up against anything that God can't heal! There isn't any problem that can't be healed; however, I do want to say something about an aspect of healing that I don't understand very well. A person can go to one healer and get no results, then go to another one, and be healed. Both healers could do it in the same way — but one will have excellent results with the client, and the other one won't! So, don't be discouraged if a healing doesn't seem to be working. Just find another healer for the client, and refer them to that healer. Maybe it's karmic that they receive their healing from someone else. There is another point to this, as well. The client may have been receiving a healing the whole time from the first healer, but the results came about at the time they went to the second healer. I have had clients whom I've sensed I was not going to be able to help. I refer them to other healers when I sense this. As I said, I don't understand this aspect of healing. I have heard other healers talk of it, too. Fortunately, since we are channels for healing, it isn't necessary that we understand everything for healing to take place, as long as we know what steps to take for the welfare of the client when it is possible for us to do so.

Question: If I'm sick, can I still channel energy?

Answer: I don't channel energy when I'm not feeling well, mainly because I don't feel I would be a clear channel.

Question: What if before or during a healing you feel tense or uptight? Will that block the healing and what do you do to relieve the tension?

Answer: I'm not sure if the healing is affected by any

41

tension inside of me. I don't think so. Usually as I am positioning myself in my chair, getting my body into a comfortable position, I take deep breaths, blowing out any stress or tension I may be feeling.

Likewise with a client, I tell them if they begin experiencing different emotions, i.e., sadness, anger, fear, etc., or become aware of feeling tense or blocked, I suggest to them that they take deep breaths (from their abdomen) and breathe out — visualizing the word release.

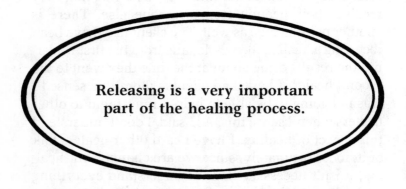

Releasing is a very important part of the healing process.

Releasing what? Releasing any old emotions, old memories, old physical and/or emotional pain. For example, if a client begins feeling a lot of sadness while I am channeling a healing to them, I tell them not to hang onto the sadness by intellectualizing it.

I suggest to clients that they "go with the emotion": let it flow, cry it out if that's what their body needs to do, or talk it out and then either silently or verbally say, "I release you, I release you."

> It is not as important
> to figure out where it comes
> from as it is important to *release*
> the emotion.

Question: Does anyone ever have a "negative" reaction to healing?

Answer: I have seen two common, what might be considered "negative" reactions to healing. However, I do not consider these negative reactions. I see them within the process of healing. When channeling healing energy, you will want to be aware of these reactions.

1. Clients with colds, emphysema, bronchitis, pneumonia, etc., may sneeze or cough more immediately after a healing because the healing has "loosened up" the infection. The coughing and sneezing is the body's way of getting rid of the "bug."

2. I have had some clients tell me they had more physical pain after the healing than before. This is usually when the person has had the physical problem (bad back, elbows, knees, feet) for a long time. I believe the pain has been in there for a long time, and the healing energy does go in where the pain is stored. So, I think it is bringing the old pain to the surface to be released. I tell the client that the pain will stop within twenty to thirty minutes after the healing. I know this because of the clients reporting back to me that it stops

44

within that amount of time. I have never had anyone call to tell me that they were still in pain an hour or two after the healing.

If a client were to call two or three hours afterward and tell me they were in pain, I would suggest they come back for another healing or would offer to send them an absentee healing.

Question: Do you believe in God? In Jesus Christ?

Answer: I certainly do.

Question: Do you feel it is necessary for **all** healers to believe in Jesus Christ?

Answer: No, I do not.

Question: Do you ever get physically ill?

Answer: Yes, I do.

Question: What religion are you?

Answer: Confirmed Presbyterian, baptized Baptist, and now a member of Unity Christ Church in Minneapolis, which is nondenominational.

Question: Do you believe people should stop going to their doctor when they are receiving a spiritual healing?

Answer: Absolutely not.

Question: Does a person have to have faith in order to be healed?

Answer: No, they don't need faith. If a client tells me they don't know if they have faith or not, I tell them I have enough for both of us. I do believe they need to want to be healed, though. I never ask a client if they have faith. That doesn't matter to me. What does matter is that they want to be healed. It is sufficient if the person just **asks** to be healed.

Question: Do your hands always get hot during a healing?

Answer: No. There have been times I have felt no energy, no heat, but the client feels both. Sometimes it's the other way around. I've done some channeling where my hands feel like they're on fire, but the client feels nothing.

Question: Is it necessary for the clients to take off their clothes?

Answer: I never ask a client to remove clothing. The healing energy flows through layers of anything.

Question: Since it's important that the person ask for the healing, is it okay to pray for a healing for someone if they don't know about it?

Answer: I can't imagine it not being okay to pray for anyone as long as I keep in mind "Thy will be done," not mine, but I would not channel an absentee healing without the person's knowledge and request for it.

Question: Is it all right to smoke during a healing?

Answer: No, I don't believe the person channeling the healing **or** the person receiving a healing should smoke during a healing. I think the people involved (healer and "healee") should focus on the healing process rather than on smoking a cigarette.

Question: Some people want to know how they can know for sure that it isn't Satan healing them.

Answer: I read somewhere in the Bible that only **God** has the power to heal, and that's what I tell people.

Question: Have you ever done a healing on an animal?

Answer:Yes, and plants, too!

Question: Is it okay to use a healing table with metal in it?

Answer: Yes. Some books may tell you it's not okay. Some may say you have to use a wooden table. Some may say you have to meditate for an hour every day or fast for two out of every seven days. Another book might say you have to use oil. Some say to stand in a south-north direction, or not to stand on cement, or not to let the client wear jewelry or digital watches, to light white candles, etc. For a while,

I was getting all caught up in these kinds of dos and don'ts,

but I have to honestly say that whether I'm following them or not, the healing energy is always the same.

Question: What is "absentee healing?"

Answer: Sending a healing to someone, usually across town, but sometimes across the country or in another part of the world. No, the channel does not have to be present in order for a person to receive a healing. Remember, it's universal energy. It's **everywhere**.

Question: How do you handle skeptics?

Answer: I used to feel I needed to defend healing, but not anymore. I believe everyone is entitled to their opinion. I listen to their beliefs, but I don't get into debates as I did sometimes in the past. I no longer try to convince people that healing works. The healing energy speaks for itself.

Question: Do you go to hospitals to do healings?

Answer: Yes, I do. Some healers I know prefer to send absentee healings in those cases, though.

Question: Does laying-on-hands healing heal emotional problems or addictions, such as alcoholism?

Answer: Addictions such as alcoholism entail more than physical problems. I believe a person suffering from any kind of major addiction is suffering physical, mental, emotional and spiritual bankruptcy, and in order to receive total healing each of these areas must be addressed. I am not a trained therapist and would not limit the client's chances to recover by pretending to be one. If a person is emotionally or mentally ill, I refer them to someone qualified to help them with that.

Question: Can I heal myself?

Answer: This question can be answered in two ways.
1. When I have been in physical pain, I have asked God to please do a healing on the problem, and I have always received the healing. I'll never forget the day I came home from the hospital after having a hysterectomy. My stomach had a 12-inch scar on it, and I was sore. I lay on my bed and asked God to please do a healing on me because I had a lot of things to do and didn't want to go through the usual six-weeks' recuperation period. I felt a deep heat through my entire body. I fell asleep. I woke up about an hour later feeling like a brand-new person. The next day I went shopping. I was back to work in only three weeks.

Receiving a healing is a wonderful experience. It's hard to describe the sense of nurturing. The loving energy is so "filling up."

2. I ask my body what the illness is trying to tell me. I am as open as possible to truly hear, see or feel what is going on inside. The more willing I am to face any emotions I may need to deal with, the easier self-healing is.

Self-healing involves honesty with yourself, above all else. You need to be willing to open yourself up to your own self, as completely as possible. **Be willing to hear, see or feel what's really going on**.

**Anyone can channel healing.
They can channel anywhere,
at any time,
In any manner they choose.**

Chapter 9

Healing Is a Process

A common myth with spiritual healing is that when healers lay their hands on people with physical problems, those people are instantly healed. I will say that this is true in some cases, but more often than not a person goes through quite a transition between their first and last healing session.

In this chapter of case studies, I will devote a small portion to healings that were instantaneous, but the larger portion, as is usually the case, will be about different processes I have seen people go through to become healed.

Mary

A woman of fifty who went into the hospital for a hysterectomy. She had been told by her doctors that her recovery time would take longer because of her age, and that she could plan on being in the hospital for at least ten days, possibly two weeks. She asked me to please come in and do a healing on her when she came out of the recovery room, and that is what I did.

I remember thinking how pale she looked. I was sure she was going to need more than just one healing, so I did a healing on her and left the hospital with that in mind. I called the hospital that night to see how she was doing and they said she'd been resting comfortably ever since she had come back from surgery. The next morning I called her room about 8:00, but there was no answer. I panicked. My human, doubtful mind was thinking all kinds of negative thoughts. I called the nurses' station to find out what happened to her, and they said she'd been up walking around since 7:00 and doing just fine. She went home three days later!

Jonathan

Jonathan was seven. For years he had recurring herpes of the mouth and chin. He was also having trouble sleeping. His mother had taken him to several doctors, but nothing was working. The herpes would come and go at random. There didn't seem to be any specific pattern.

I placed a white handkerchief on his lips and chin, and did a healing. He slept hard for almost one hour. When he awoke, the herpes was still there. His mother called the next day to say the herpes was gone.

I was told by his guides during the healing that every night when he went to bed he needed to listen to some very calming music. His guides* told me he was psychically very sensitive and would "pick up" all kinds of things throughout a day, and that this would

---

* "Guides" refers to friends and helpers who exist on the spirit plane, but are not present in a physical body. They can offer assistance and advice if we are open to asking and to "hearing" a response.

make him very hyper by bedtime.

I spoke with his mother several months later, and she told me that Jonathan was very faithful about listening to meditation-type music tapes every night at bedtime and that the herpes had never recurred after that one healing.

Arleen

Arleen had a staph infection in her eyes. Both eyes were beet-red, very full of pus and very swollen. She had gone to an eye specialist who told her the infection was so bad, he was concerned she might lose the sight in one of her eyes. He gave her some medication and told her to come back every day until it cleared up.

She called me that night, and I went over to her home. I had never seen anything like it. Her eyes were a mess. Any light was very painful, so she kept her sunglasses on. I had her sit up in a chair. I put a white handkerchief and my left hand on the back of her head. The energy started flowing immediately. The eyes were draining like nobody's business! She was busy with tissues while I was praying for the healing. My right hand would fill up with a sharp pain, and then it would leave. Fill up and leave. Fill up and leave. This went on for about fifteen minutes. After about twenty minutes of healing, the energy stopped.

I was just about to ask her if she wanted me to come back the next day, when my inner voice told me it wouldn't be necessary. So, I did ask her if she would call me and let me know how she was doing. She called me the next afternoon after she had come home from the doctor's. She said the doctor was totally amazed at how her eyes had improved. She said he even called in one of the nurses to show her how well Arleen was doing. Arleen was amazed. The infection was almost gone. The draining had stopped. The redness had cleared up. I guess my inner voice knew what it was talking about!

Ted

Ted and his back. One night I had a date with a man who understood very little about what I do professionally. He was about fifteen minutes late. When he got to my home, he was moving very slowly and it was obvious he was in a lot of pain. He said he had pulled something in his back that afternoon while playing racquetball. I told him I could do a healing on his back if he wanted, but he was noticeably uncomfortable at the suggestion. He said we were late and that we'd better get going. We were due at a dinner party in ten minutes, so we left. But, on the way there, he asked me what "this healing stuff" was all about. I explained as much as I could in the limited time, but as we talked, my right hand began to heat up, and I could feel that it was "full" of energy. Even though he asked me questions, I could sense there was a part of him that didn't want to hear the answers.

As we walked up the stairs to our friends' house, Ted made the comment that maybe if the evening didn't get too late, I could do "one of those healings" on him. My right hand went right to the spot in his back that was in pain, and a huge bolt of energy came out of my hand. The energy was so intense it actually knocked him forward about a foot. He said, "What the hell was that!?" And I told him that was the healing energy.

Our friends were at their front door at that point, so we didn't discuss it further but went in. About halfway through dinner, Ted looked over at me in utter amazement and whispered that it had just occurred

to him that his back hadn't hurt since we walked in the door!

George

George, fifty-eight years old, had several blockages in the arteries around his heart. He was taking several nitroglycerin tablets each day to stay alive. According to his doctor he was given three to six months to live, and when he called me he was on his last month. He said he had nothing to lose, and wanted to give spiritual healing a try.

The first week I saw him three times. He was able to cut down on his nitroglycerin by a considerable amount. There were some days when he didn't need any. His color was improving. His breathing was better. For the next three weeks I saw him twice a week, and for about two months I saw him once a week.

When I first started seeing George, he was a pretty gruff, unfriendly guy: sarcastic, critical of others. He seemed to have a "holier-than-thou" attitude. I saw psychically that he had a tremendous amount of fear. No, this fear was not of death. It was a fear of getting close to other people. He treated others gruffly so they wouldn't get too close. He was like a big, spoiled child. Over the weeks, I talked to him about his sarcasm and his fears. We talked about his relationships with family members and the importance of healing those relationships.

He slowly began changing his attitudes. He became more considerate of others, more loving, more sensitive. A total change was taking place, and it was wonderful to witness. Each time we did a healing, we would open up a little bit more. I saw him for a total of three months. He lived a fairly active life (without nitroglycerin) for one more year.

Kathryn

Kathryn: this client taught me quite a bit. She was twenty-six years old. She had cancer in her right breast. The lump was underneath her arm. The first time I met her, I placed my hand under her armpit. The tumor was as big as my palm. She was sure she was going to be healed and back to perfect health.

I met with her once a week for about three months. She was always showing improvement. The tumor was smaller each time I saw her. We had become very close. We were about the same age and had similar life experiences.

One day after a healing session, we talked about what her life was going to be like when she was completely healed. We talked about her old job, the relationships with her boyfriend and her family. We talked about all the things she hadn't been able to do for so long and about her anxiety and fears of "returning to the normal world."

At about the end of the third month, I went on vacation for two weeks, and when I got back I got a call from a mutual friend of ours who said that Kathryn had become very ill and wanted to see me as soon as possible. I jumped in the car and went to her home. She was lying on the couch, moaning in pain. She had lumps all over her neck. I had to pick her up and roll her over because she was too weak to do it herself. I was overwhelmed. I felt so helpless. I couldn't stand seeing her in such pain. I prayed hard for answers, and I was feeling so guilty because I had left her for two weeks.

I went to her home the next couple of days and did more healings, but lumps were popping up everywhere. My inner voice kept saying something about a "fast," but I didn't understand what that meant.

About the third day I asked her if she had fasted while I was in San Francisco. She said she had decided to clean out her system, so that she had gone on an apple-and-water fast for those two weeks! She had lost thirteen pounds.

I was so angry. I was hurt. For weeks I had felt a real sense of comradeship with her in her healing process, and I felt like that was gone. She was no longer there with me. Why? Why had she done this to herself? The fast seemed like she was starving herself — and such a contradiction to the healthy body we were striving for.

Don't misunderstand me. I'm not saying there's anything wrong with fasting — what I **am** saying is that the fast ''felt'' very inappropriate as far as timing in this case. We were really making what appeared to be progress, and it seemed to me that in order to continue with the ''flow'' we were in, she needed to give her body proper nourishment. I realized at that point that I had become far too emotionally involved and that I had to separate our friendship from what was happening. Another part to all of this was that her family was becoming quite upset with me. They felt I was killing her. They didn't want me around her any more. She went to the hospital, and died two weeks later.

A mutual friend called me to tell me to stay away from the funeral, and that the family was acting like they were on a ''witch hunt'' and were just waiting for me to show up.

I didn't go to the funeral. I was dealing with my own grief and confusion. I was angry with God. I was angry with Kathryn. I was angry that I even had this gift, and I told God that I was through. I would never do another healing as long as I lived. He needed someone tougher than I was — that was clear to me.

Two days later, I got a call from a friend of mine.

Her stepson had fallen eighteen feet and landed on his head. He had been in a coma for weeks down in Nebraska, and they were flying him up to one of our major hospital centers. She asked if I would please do healings on him when he arrived in Minnesota.

But before I continue with this example, and how I returned to using the gift of channeling healings, I would like to share with you the important lessons I learned from working with Kathryn.

Remember, You Are the Channel

1. It is important to stay detached from my clients. I can love them, care about them, but when I become personally involved, I lose a certain amount of good judgment that I believe is necessary to be a clear, noninterfering channel for healing.

2. It is important to always remember I am not responsible for the outcome of anyone's healing process, no matter how it turns out. I am the channel for it, not the power, itself.

3. Though I may think I know what is right for another person, in reality I cannot judge what other people need, or what is right for them. Again, **I am a channel for healing energy, and that's it**!

4. It is important to remember that going from a restricted life style due to bad health to a nonrestricted life style with good health can be devastating to some people. Going from a long illness to good health is a major change and, definitely a **process**.

5. It is important to be grateful for each healing rather than always to be looking to the "end results."

I don't know what the "end result" should be for any other person. I am a channel for God's healing energy.

6. Last, but not least, it is possible that death is a healing for some people, and it is not my place to judge that.

And now, back to Gary's story . . .

Gary

Gary, age fourteen. As I told you earlier, Gary had been in a coma for about four weeks when they flew him up from Nebraska to one of our major medical centers. I was still grieving Kathryn's death and did not want to do any more healings. Actually, I was afraid. I knew Gary's family fairly well. I guess you could say I had become gun shy. I was full of doubt and confusion. What if he died like Kathryn did? What if the family then held me responsible? I went in circles for a day, praying and yet not wanting to hear what my inner voice said.

His family called several times to ask if I was willing to work with him. Then one morning when I was in the shower and my mind wasn't on any one thing in particular, out of "nowhere" I got a very clear vision of Gary lying in the hospital. I saw me sitting next to him with my hands on him, and my inner voice then said, "go!" With that came a real desire to do just that. So, within a couple of hours I was at the hospital. I have to admit to you that this was about seven years ago, and I don't remember all the details of Gary's recovery. But, there are some I remember clearly that I think will be helpful to you when you are working with someone in a coma.

First off, when I arrived, a male nurse was telling the family that he doubted that Gary would ever come

out of the coma, and that if by chance he did, he would very likely be unable to speak, walk or ever take care of himself. He suggested that the family put him in a nursing home. That old doubt started creeping up in me. Right there I had to decide if I was going to hang on to the bleak diagnosis of the medical establishment or set myself apart from it and just do my job. I decided to leave the negativity outside of Gary's room and to go for the healing energy.

First things first. I couldn't communicate with him, so I ran my hands down his body about two inches above it, feeling for cold spots in his aura. Cold spots indicate where there's a problem with the body. There were cold spots, everywhere. I prayed for direction. My inner voice directed me all the time.

About the third day of healings, I experienced something new. Gary's soul stepped out of his body and communicated with me. It was great! His soul knew every need that his body had. About the fifth day, his body started to respond. There was movement in his arms and legs. He was moaning a little bit. The sixth day the doctors said they needed to operate on him. They said they needed to put a kind of bypass in his brain because the spinal fluids were not draining properly and the fluid was building up in his head. They said that without this device he would die. But, his soul told me that his body was not strong enough for surgery, so I was to concentrate on putting a lot of energy everywhere to get him stronger. They wanted to do surgery that afternoon, and I was really worried that he wouldn't be strong enough. My inner voice, however, told me to calm down, that everything would be fine.

That afternoon, about an hour before they were going to take him to surgery, a strange substance showed up in his blood. My first thought was, "What the heck

61

is going on?" My inner voice told me again that everything was going to be fine and to just concentrate on getting his body stronger.

They called all his relatives to the hospital to test their blood for this strange new substance. They couldn't operate until they could identify it. No one knew what it was. They postponed surgery.

I did about three more healings in the meantime. The next day my inner voice told me that he was strong enough to go through surgery. That morning, the strange substance mysteriously disappeared.

The operation was successful. The spinal fluids were flowing through the bypass. I continued to go to the hospital each day for about a week. Gary had come out of the coma. His speech was fine. He walked with a walker. He had a lot of adjustments to make: his pituitary gland had been permanently damaged, so he would need to take medication every day for that. He developed diabetes while in the coma. His vision was gone in one of his eyes. When I was working with his eyes, I saw a picture of blackness behind the eyeball. Blackness. It felt as if there was nothing there at all. The family told me when he was in Nebraska, the doctors had severed the nerves going to that eye because of a buildup of pressure. No wonder I was getting blackness! There was nothing there to work with.

Gary stayed in the hospital for about another month — mainly for rehabilitation. His legs needed to get stronger. He had trouble swallowing food. After he was out of the coma, I went to the hospital another three times. Then it felt as if the healing was finished. I saw him about six months later. He was doing fairly well. He lived at home, he was back in school. The strange thing was that neither one of us knew the other six months later. He had gained weight. His hair had all grown back. Until his mother introduced me, I didn't know that the young man walking around the kitchen talking baseball was Gary!

Dan

Dan was nineteen years old. He dove into a swimming hole, which turned out to be about three feet deep. He smashed his spinal cord. He was paralyzed from the neck down.

He had been vacationing with family and friends on the West Coast when the accident happened. He had been in the hospital for about three days before I got the first call from his family to please send absentee healings. Whenever I do an absentee healing, I ask God for the healing, visualize it being done, and I end with: "Thank you, Father." With Dan, I did this three times a day.

We were about 2,000 miles apart but I felt a strong connection with Dan. I really had a strong feeling to go out there and work on him directly but didn't have that kind of money. I prayed for an answer. The next day his family called to say they wanted to pay my way out there if I would be willing to come, so I canceled all appointments and took off for Oregon for the week.

I went to the hospital twice a day for the first three days. I placed my hands on his solar plexus when he was lying on his back. When they turned him over, we worked on his neck and spine. About the fourth day, he got a very bad bladder infection and a high fever, so for the next couple of days we worked on his bladder and worked a little on his arms and legs to get the energy flowing. About the fifth day, the bladder infection cleared up. He was beginning to raise his arms by himself. I continued to work on his neck, spine and solar plexus. The seventh day found him feeling much better. He wiggled his right foot for me and was waving his arms around. His appetite returned. He was doing much better, mentally. The week went fast. It was time for me to get back to work in Minneapolis. I never saw Dan again, but I have gotten reports from his family that he left the hospital much earlier than was expected. He did not regain the use of his legs, and he uses a wheelchair. He is in college, has his own apartment and, according to his family, he is doing great.

Sharon

Sharon, age thirty-two, had genital herpes. Sharon's healing process was a little more involved than just physical healing. The first time she came for a healing, I placed my hands on her solar plexus and asked the energy to go wherever the body needed healing. I was told by my inner voice she needed to forgive the person who had given her the herpes and to forgive herself for contracting the disease. She had a lot of shame and guilt locked up inside. I was told she needed to release these negative feelings about herself. She came back a week later for another healing. My inner voice said she still needed to release more negative feelings toward herself and the person she contracted the herpes from, so I suggested she pray every day for forgiveness and again for the release of her negative feelings. I did another healing on her solar plexus, praying for the energy to completely heal the herpes.

Next, I suggested she stop referring to the herpes as "my" herpes, but rather to refer to it as "the" herpes. The last suggestion I gave her was something I had learned at my church called "Affirm and Deny." I suggested that she **deny** the herpes if it recurred. Most people with herpes can feel the onset of a breakout by sensations of burning, itching and tingling. I told her that if she felt anything like these onset sensations, to

affirm, "**I deny this herpes**," thereby taking the power away from the disease.

Sharon called several months later to say she had not had any herpes since our last session.

Denying the Disease

I am not saying this denial works in every case, but it can work. God can heal anything, if it should be healed. But the suggestions given to Sharon were pretty powerful. Forgiveness. Not owning the disease by referring to it as "mine," and taking the power of the illness away by denying it. Don't misunderstand me! I'm not saying to deny it in the sense of hiding your head in the sand and pretending it's not there. I mean, don't affirm the condition or its power . . . affirm instead your rejection of the condition's existence.

Think of it this way. Let's say someone you don't particularly care for shows up at your front door with luggage. This person informs you that they intend to visit you for ten days. Would you say, "Sure, come on in, I'll rearrange my whole schedule for you"? Or, would you put your foot down and say, "Sorry, I just can't accommodate you at this time." Hopefully you would be firm about it and not allow yourself to have this intrusion forced on you. Sound silly to compare something like this to herpes? An intrusion is an intrusion! Just put your foot down, and tell those little cold sores they aren't welcome. Deny them. Don't affirm them.

Patty

Patty was in her forties. She had back problems. She called me one day in very bad pain. Her back was really

bothering her. She couldn't bend over and could bare-
ly walk.

She couldn't get an appointment immediately with
her chiropractor and wanted to come right over for an
emergency healing.

I placed one hand on her lower back and one hand
on her upper back. She cried during most of the healing, not because of the physical pain, but because she
was feeling so much sadness. My inner voice said she
was carrying old memories of her whole life in her
back, that she was far too burdened with the past.

After the healing, she felt physically better and
emotionally drained. It felt like she needed to release
a lot of old emotions. I suggested that every time she
had an old memory or felt an emotion, she pray for
it to be released. I told her that sometimes taking big,
deep breaths and blowing them out will release blocked
energy.

She called two days later for another healing. When
she got here, she said that she had become aware that
her difficulty stemmed as much if not more from
spiritual trouble than from physical difficulty with her
back, and she asked for a spiritual healing. So this time
I put both hands on her solar plexus, which is where
we store so much emotion. I prayed that the energy
go wherever the body needed it.

Patty called me later that night and we talked for
quite a while about what more she needed to do. She
told me she had many papers filled with memories of
the past stored around her house. We came to the con-
clusion that maybe it was necessary to gather all these
papers and burn them in the fireplace. Patty was really anxious to be healed, and to do whatever was
necessary. She came for another healing two days later
and I could see the difference in her face before she
told me that the cleaning-out process was really a

67

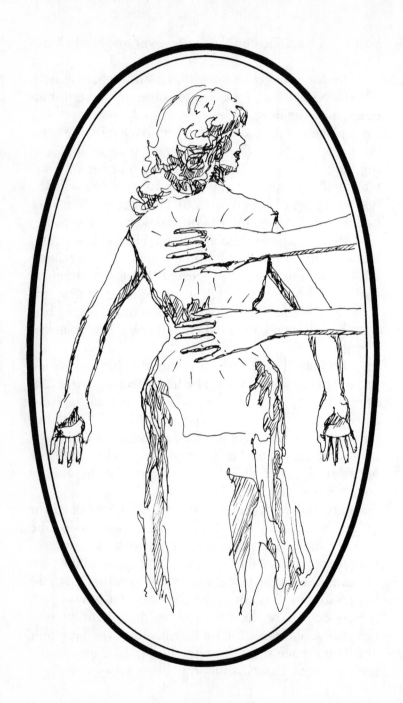

healing in itself, or part of the whole process of healing. Recently I saw her and she said she's still going through her "cleaning out the old" process, and that her back was feeling so much better.

Patty came to me for a healing because she was at that time part of one of my psychic classes. Her need to know more about her psychic aspect, and specifically about healing, caused her to take the class. So, when she came for her own healing, she was very involved in the need for transformation and change, but had come to a near standstill despite her involvement in class and reading as much as she could in the area.

The load of old hurts she carried in her back was literally immobilizing her. But going through the pain and the process of healing awakened her and assisted her along on her spiritual path. It showed her, in a way she couldn't ignore any longer, that she needed to clear away the past before she could move ahead spiritually. It showed her that the path of spiritual development is more than intellectual how-to, and that it involves everything that a person is: spirit, emotions, mind and body. She learned that only when these things are unified is progress made for the soul.

I hear from Patty these days that her own activity in channeling healings is growing fast. Her changes are no longer blocked as they were. She tells me that when she experiences blockage again, she will have more understanding about what might be causing it, and that she will know more about how to get help for it. She tells me that the process of channeling healing for other people is actually something that heals and teaches her.

Judy

Judy, age thirty, said she felt a coldness in her abdomen. When she first came for a healing, she said she felt disconnected from herself. She was also low on energy. In general she was feeling all out-of-sorts but couldn't put her finger on anything specific.

I have done several healings on clients who come for an energy boost. I lay my hands on the solar plexus, do a twenty-minute healing and pray to fill up the entire body with white light. Afterward, I put a **spiritual shield** on the solar plexus, having been directed to do so by my inner voice.

My friends refer to this spiritual shield as "the **psychic bandage**." It is done in this way: I hold my hands next to one another and circle over the solar plexus about two inches above the body. I move my hands counter clockwise. Sometimes I keep the left hand on the body and use my right hand to circle the solar plexus. I go round and round five to ten times until it "feels complete."

A number of my clients are therapists. Often, because of the nature of their work and because they open themselves up so much to their clients' troubles, it gets to be too much and they end up feeling scattered or "burned out." Several have commented on how much clearer they feel after coming for a spiritual shield healing. They don't feel so vulnerable. They don't exhaust their energy as they did before.

So when Judy told me what her needs were, I just figured it would be a one-time energy boost healing, ending with a psychic bandage. One of these days I'll learn! Once the healing began to flow, I could see Judy's uterus, very shriveled up and cold. It felt very cold. Judy cried through most of the healing. Psychically it felt as though we had only just begun a process that was going to take quite some time.

Judy started coming every week for healings. Several different things were happening. She got in touch with her anger about being a woman. She

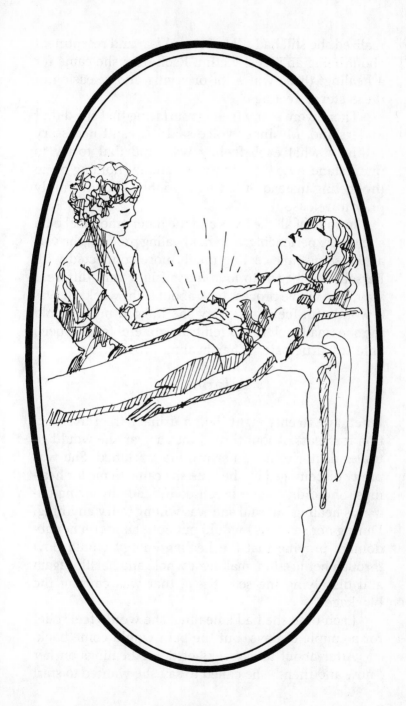

71

realized she still had a lot of stored fear and resentment about being an incest victim. Each time she came for a healing, there was a lot of crying and releasing of these stored feelings.

There were many feelings surfacing that she didn't understand. My inner voice said it wasn't necessary to know what each feeling was, and that to try to understand **every** feeling was actually holding on to the feeling instead of letting it go. She should simply pray to release it.

In spite of all the tears and the inner emotional pain she was experiencing with her healing process, she was at the same time feeling much more connected with herself. She began to love herself in a very different way. The whole process took about eight weeks. It was a wonderful feeling the day she hugged me and told me she finally felt free. I felt truly grateful to have been able to participate in her healing process.

Janet

Janet, age twenty-eight, had a urinary tract dysfunction for years. About three times a year she would go to her doctor to have her urethra stretched. She was pretty discouraged by the time she came to me for healings. She didn't have much confidence in laying-on-hands healing but said she was willing to try anything. During her sessions I would put both hands on her abdomen, praying that the healing energy would flow through her urethra, making it whole and healthy again and dissolving the scar tissue that was causing the blockage.

Each time she had a healing, she would feel relief for a couple of days, but the pain would come back.

After about four weeks of doing healings on her "now and then," she called to say she wanted to start coming regularly until the problem was cleared up. I told her I would send absentee healings until we met again. That night as I was praying for a healing, my inner voice said she did not feel worthy of being healed. I was rather surprised, because I thought I knew this woman pretty well, and it didn't seem to fit her. But I did call her in the morning to ask her about it. She immediately started to cry when I mentioned the word "worthy." She said that she did not feel worthy and that throughout the healings she had been afraid because she felt God was angry with her. She felt that some things she had done in the past had caused God to be angry with her and that her physical problem was her punishment. She actually feared that God would make her problem worse!

We talked for quite a while on the phone that morning. The words that came to me during this were: "Ask her to pray to feel worthy of healing."

I told her I would pray for her fear to be removed and asked her to pray that she feel worthy of being a healthy person. We left it that when she was feeling worthy, she would get back to me. Three days later she called to say that she was ready, that she had done a lot of praying in those three days and that something inside her had changed .

I met with her that afternoon. The healing was quite unusual and I think you'll find it very interesting. I placed my right hand on her abdomen. The heat came immediately. After about five minutes it literally felt like my hand had gone inside her stomach. It was the strangest sensation. I tried pulling my hand off her, but it was stuck as if it had been glued to her. She opened her eyes and yelled, "Your hand is inside me!" I told her that I could feel the same thing but that it was not inside. It was just stuck on her abdomen.

My inner voice was reassuring. It told me

everything was fine and to just do my part. She and I could both feel "rearranging" going on inside. It was an amazing thing to feel. After about seven minutes we could both feel the hand slip out of her body, the energy stop flowing, and my hand become free to move. We both sat there in shock. We didn't know what to make of it. We sat and talked for quite a long while and when I felt she was okay, I left. We have seen each other several times over the last few years and she always tells me she's "still fine." After that healing that day, she has never had another problem with her urethra. That was the only experience I ever had with that kind of a healing.

Bob

Bob was in his fifties. He had lost his job. He came for one healing because of depression. After the session he said he didn't want to spend any more money on this, so would I please send absentee healings. I said I would. I prayed for three days for healing on his depression. The fourth day Bob called. He wanted to know if I was still sending the healing. I told him that I was. He asked me to please stop. He said, "Things are starting to happen to force me to face my depression." He said he was kind of surprised, because he really hadn't expected it to work. But, since it was working, would I please stop since he didn't think he was ready to deal with all of it.

I felt badly for Bob because he seemed stuck in such a heavy place emotionally, but I stopped praying for absentee healing to him.

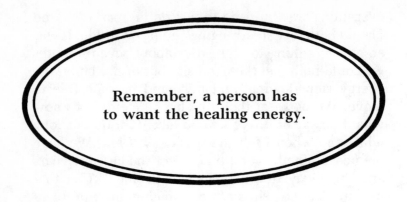

Remember, a person has
to want the healing energy.

Grace

Grace was full of arthritis. It was crippling her entire
body. She came weekly for healings for about three
weeks. Her fingers were straightening out a bit. She
was able to walk a little without her cane. Her energy
was returning. One day she started to cry during the
session. My inner voice said her body was actually crying because of what the arthritis had done to her. It
was truly an emotional session for her. When she left,
she said she'd call, but I had a strong feeling that she
wasn't coming back.

I could feel Grace was very embarrassed about crying in front of me. It felt like she was very afraid of
her sadness. My sense was that she did not want to
go any further with the healing process because she
did not want to look at her body and its pain that close-
ly. Some people would rather stay in denial of anything
that is going on emotionally with them. They may feel
victimized by their illness but fear facing their emotions even more.

Grace did not come back.

Ben

Ben had a heart attack about a year before I met him and was starting to have chest pains again. He was really very badly frightened. He didn't want to have another attack. He was a very sweet and gentle man, very respectful of healing.

The night I met with Ben and his wife, we first started to talk about healing energy and about our spiritual beliefs. I felt a certain apprehension from his wife but decided not to let it bother me. I prayed for a bubble of protection* because I did not want to feel any of her negativity.

I placed both of my hands on Ben's chest. The healing energy was very intense. Ben cried quietly during the healing. He said he knew that God was healing him. He was so thankful afterwards and said he would call if he needed more. The next day I got a very brief phone call from Ben telling me that his wife was very concerned because I am not a "Charismatic," and he was sorry, but he couldn't come for any more healings. Needless to say, I was pretty upset. It doesn't make sense to me when religion interferes with God's healing. No, I didn't express anger to Ben. My anger wasn't his problem. It was mine.

Henry

Henry was eighty-three years old when I met him. He wanted healing for chest pains and a low energy level. Every week for about five weeks Henry's wife, Mary, would drive him sixty miles to get his "treatment." He was a quiet man and very respectful of healing. He

---

* Whenever you feel the need, you can visualize yourself surrounded by a large, clear bubble which lets air, love and all life's nutrients in — but keeps negativity out. Some people visualize themselves surrounded in white light for a similar effect.

never had much to say except to let me know he was feeling better. After our fifth visit together, Henry told me he felt he was healed. He said he was feeling like a young man of sixty. His chest pains were gone. His energy level was back up to where he wanted it to be. He told me he'd call if he had a need for any more healing. Every year I receive a Christmas card from Henry and Mary, always with a note that Henry is doing just fine.

Jerry

Jerry was sixteen years old when I met him. He was born with cerebral palsy. I remember clearly the fear I felt inside of me the night he walked up to me on crutches and asked me if I could heal his legs. He said he wanted to ride a horse, drive a car and be like everybody else. I explained to him that the healing energy came from God, and that I needed to pray about it.

The fear I felt was that his condition might be *karmic*, and if it was, perhaps he was not ready to be physically healed. I believe God's will for Jerry was for him to walk free of the crutches and to live a "normal" life; but again, I believe Jerry's soul chose the cerebral palsy and because of that I didn't know what to do. I assumed that because he was asking for the healing, perhaps he was done with the *karmic* lesson. But, as you know by now, my assumptions have not always been right, so I took it to God. I asked for a clear sign. Was Jerry to receive healing or not? The next morning I awoke with a vision of my hands on Jerry's legs, so I called him and we set up our first appointment.

Our first session was pretty uncomfortable. Jerry's mother was quite negative. She was sure her son would not be healed. In spite of her constant negative remarks, I continued to channel healings on Jerry's legs for about four weeks.

During this time I became aware of an American Indian spirit named **White Horse** working with me. I would channel energy into Jerry's head, and White Horse would stand at his feet pulling the energy down.

There were so many breaks in the flow of Jerry's energy. Each week Jerry would give me a progress report. He felt his legs were getting stronger. He felt a lot of tingling in his legs. He was always so enthusiastic.

About the fifth week a friend of mine who also channels healing asked if he could work on Jerry with me, so together we worked on Jerry's legs, feet, the flow of energy in his body and his upper torso. Several weeks passed from the first day I lay my hands on Jerry's legs. Slowly we saw progress. We were all very excited. The night Jerry stood and took a few steps without his crutches, we all cheered.

In all the weeks we worked together and talked about Jerry's expectations of his future without crutches, it had **never** occurred to me that this drastic change in his life style could be threatening to him mentally and emotionally. We talked to Jerry for quite a while about what life without crutches might be like. People would no longer think of him as "crippled." The expectations he might have and others might have of him would change. We were so close and yet something inside suddenly didn't feel right. My inner voice told me to back off and to give Jerry time to really think about his old way of life versus a new way of life. We told Jerry to think everything over very clearly and to let us know if he wanted to continue with healings. He never called me back.

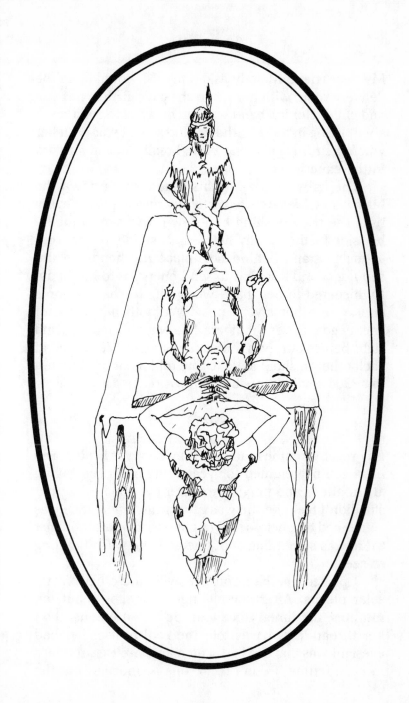

Melody

My dear friend Melody asked me if I would be in the delivery room with her when she gave girth to her second child. Her husband was too nervous to even think about being in there with her, and since I was with her when their first child was born, I really looked forward to the experience.

The baby was taking his time coming down the birth canal. Melody's face literally turned purple every time she tried pushing him down. I was standing by her side feeling totally helpless. It suddenly occurred to me to stand behind her, place my hands on her shoulders and ask God to send energy into her body. I whispered to her that I was going to channel some energy into her and — **pow**! We both felt a bolt of energy go into her shoulders. She was able to relax, and right before our eyes, out came Shawn. We looked at each other in sheer delight. She told me it literally felt like God lovingly pushed Shawn out!

Kay

Kay recently came to me wanting her eyes healed. She has been nearsighted for years. She had been saying affirmations and praying that her eyes be healed, but she didn't feel like she was getting anywhere. She was concerned that her poor eyesight was an indication that there was something about herself she wasn't willing to see.

I placed one hand on her eyes, the other on her solar plexus. After channeling energy for about ten minutes, my inner voice told me to put one hand on her throat area. I was told the **real** root of her bad eyesight was that she had seen many unpleasant things in her lifetime. I don't think this is unusual. But the

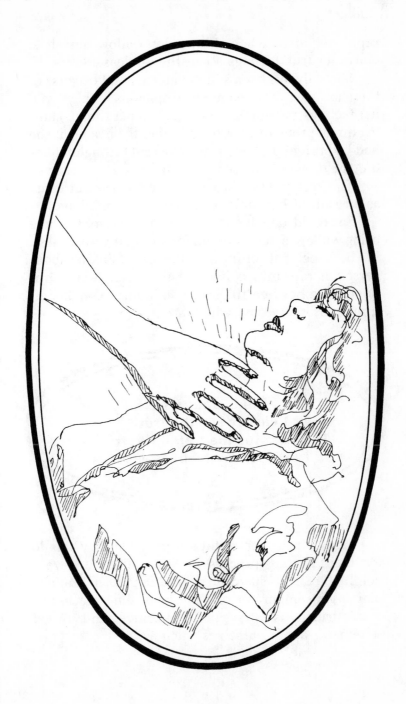

problem started when she wouldn't allow herself to voice her true feelings about the unpleasantness.

She's always been somewhat shy, and because of this she's always stifled her true opinions. "They" said her feelings and opinions get stuck in her throat, causing throat problems. I asked her after the healing if she had had throat problems, and she said throughout her life she'd been bothered with them.

The eyes and the throat were really being affected as a result of her inability to voice her opinions.

She decided to discontinue the healings for the time being while she hunts around for an assertiveness class. We both feel that getting over the fear of talking about herself, her feelings, opinions, beliefs, etc., is **very important to her health**. She's continuing to say her affirmations every day, which are:

> I like what I see.
> I clearly see the truth.
> It is safe for me to tell the truth.
> I express my feelings easily.

Many times clients will ask me what they can do for their healing processes. Affirmations are very helpful. I really believe our attitude and visualizations play a very important role in our healing process.

Affirmations are simple, positive and direct statements about ourselves, such as:

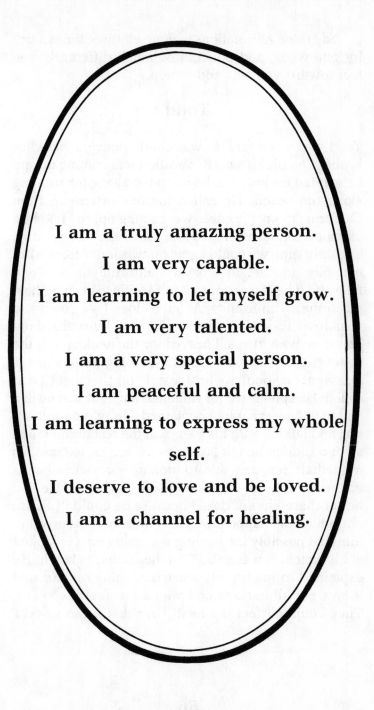

I am a truly amazing person.

I am very capable.

I am learning to let myself grow.

I am very talented.

I am a very special person.

I am peaceful and calm.

I am learning to express my whole
self.

I deserve to love and be loved.

I am a channel for healing.

Say these affirmations to yourself three times a day for one week, and notice how much differently you feel toward yourself and others.

Todd

Todd was a runner. He was coming once a week for healings on his knees. His vacation was coming up and he wanted his knees to be in tip-top shape for running along the beach. He called me one afternoon from California to say his knees were acting up, so I told him I would channel healing to him sometime that evening. The only time we could agree on was ten o'clock Minneapolis time (eight o'clock California time). Todd knew he'd be in a restaurant in San Diego at eight, having dinner with friends. At ten o'clock I sat down and visualized Todd sitting in a restaurant. I visualized my hands on both knees. I prayed for the healing, felt the connection. I thanked God for healing Todd's knees and went on about my business. Later that night Todd called. He apologized for calling so late, but said he just had to tell me what had happened. He said he was sitting and talking with his friends at the restaurant when all of a sudden he felt hands on his knees. He said his immediate reaction was to look at everyone's hands on the table, to see who was "playing around." He said he sat there kind of dazed because he couldn't figure out what was happening. He said it then occurred to him that possibly the healing was going on. He looked at his watch. It was 8:02. Then he started to laugh. He explained to his friends what was going on. He said they were all curious and wanted to feel his knees. They could all feel the heat! Isn't that a fun story?

Jack

I share this next story with you in the hope that you'll read it and learn from it. I was pretty new at all this when I started channeling energy to Jack. I hadn't learned about detachment yet, or about my own boundaries. I was still with the impression that all healings were supposed to **heal** a person totally. It hadn't occurred to me that the healing energy might simply be used to help a person be comfortable while they were in their death process.

One of my closest friend's father, Jack, had heart surgery, and during the surgery he had suffered a stroke. On my way to the hospital I was praying for a sign as to what to do. I didn't get much of a feeling about anything. I didn't get yes, I didn't get no. His family desperately wanted him to be healed. I became emotionally involved right away. I saw the fear on their faces. "I" wanted to fix the situation. For the most part, I dropped everything in my own life and went to the hospital every day. A couple of times when he would go back on the critical list I would stay overnight at the hospital. I didn't separate myself at all. I stayed emotionally hooked in with everyone else. Each day we would see some progress and by the next day something else would go wrong.

I remember clearly on a Sunday afternoon I was sitting next to his bed channeling a healing when my solar plexus suddenly started jerking. It felt like something was ripping my insides out. I couldn't get it to stop. I prayed for an understanding of what was happening. I heard someone walk up behind me. It was the spirit I mentioned earlier: White Horse. He told me to get out of the room, get out of the hospital. He was very firm. He repeated it over and over. After seeing White Horse during many of the healings I had channeled, I had come to trust what he had to say. So I got up and left the room. I couldn't walk standing straight. I was hunched over in pain, my solar plexus continuing to jerk. I went down to the family room and told my friend I had to get out of the hospital. She called a psychic in town and asked him if he knew what the jerking was. The psychic said I was channeling my own life's energy to Jack and that I had become so involved with him that I was giving up my own energy to keep him alive.

If you skimmed over that last paragraph, **please go back and read it again**. It was a frightening experience, and one I hope you won't have to go through. I left the hospital. I went home and went to bed. That afternoon the family called to say Jack had a heart attack. They asked me if I would please come up to the hospital. My inner voice said **no** — very loudly. The next day I went to a healer friend of mine to get a healing on myself. He helped me to see what I was doing. He told me I had to detach myself, that I was not responsible for Jack's wellness, that I couldn't allow myself to be affected by what everyone wanted for Jack. He told me that maybe Jack's soul was trying to leave his body. Those were some important words for me to hear.

I continued to channel energy to Jack for about four more days. I was not channeling the energy with that desperate feeling of "**Live!**" I was channeling the energy to relieve the physical pain he was in. On a Thursday afternoon I went to the hospital to do a healing on him. I placed my hands on his chest and nothing came out of my hands. My inner voice told me Jack had made his decision and that he would be leaving his body, soon. He passed away that night.

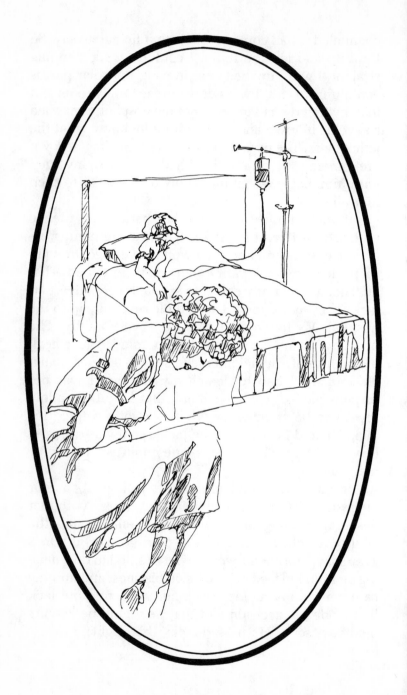

We Don't Have All the Answers

I'd like to say a little more here about the flow of energy. There will be times when you'll put your hands on someone to channel a healing, and nothing will come. Don't panic. Don't assume it means something negative. It could simply mean they don't need a healing that day. I've had clients come for healings three and four days in a row, and maybe the second or third day nothing flows from my hands; but then the next day the energy flows again. I don't know why, for sure. It's another one of those reminders that we are not in control — and we as channels **don't have all the answers**.

As I have already said in this book, this work can sometimes be very frustrating. I know in my heart that God's healing energy works. I also have learned that we humans can get in the way of that energy. We try to intellectualize the process, analyze the energy. We judge it, according to our preset beliefs, and many times because of our fears. We can't actually **see** it or **measure** it so we doubt it, ridicule it, minimize it or deny it.

Won't it be wonderful when we stop judging the healing energy and just accept its existence? We accept radio waves, and we can't see those.

So many of us believe healings and miracles were possible when Jesus Christ was walking the earth, but in the twentieth century, for some reason, many people don't believe it's possible. And I'm talking about people who pride themselves on their church attendance every Sunday!

What do you think? Or, maybe I should reword that. What do you feel about spiritual healing? What does your inner voice say? That voice is there. Just waiting to talk to you!

91

Chapter 10

Dependency

Once in a while you may find one of your clients becoming dependent on you. I have had many people throughout the years tell me they didn't want to be completely healed because then they couldn't keep coming for healings. They love receiving the nurturing they feel from being touched. For some people, receiving laying-on-hands healing is the only time they are touched in a loving way.

This has always been a difficult situation for me to deal with. I had to tell one client that I would not channel any more healings to her — and it was very difficult for me to say that. She was a woman in her middle thirties. She was a therapist. Her job was very stressful. She didn't know how to get her own needs met in a healthy way. Her way of getting love was by getting sick. She would get a lot of attention from her husband and friends every time she got another illness. By the time she first came to me for healings, she had had over a dozen operations. It took me a while to see what was going on, but one evening I finally understood.

She had been coming for a lump in her arm which the doctors felt should be surgically removed. The lump disappeared after a few healings, but then she called to say that the doctors had told her she was going blind. That night while I was working on her eyes, I checked out clairvoyantly what was happening to her body. I saw pictures of a past life where she had been crippled. She had a lot of nurturing and a lot of love in that lifetime. I saw a sadness inside of her because she missed the nurturing, the touching, the love. Subconsciously, the only way she knew how to get what she needed physically and emotionally was to be sick.

I told her about the images I had seen after I finished the healing. She told me that asking the people in her life to give her what she needed from them emotionally terrified her. She said the only way she ever got any attention from her mother was when she was sick. We talked about the stress on her job, the stress in her marriage, her relationship with her son. I asked her to please give a lot of thought to finding new and healthy ways to get the love and attention she was needing so badly.

We did a few more healings on her eyes and the problem cleared up. About a month later, she wanted to come for healings on her legs because they were getting arthritic. After her legs were healed, she called for healings on her breasts. She told me she had had surgery on them and needed to get healed from the surgery in order to get back to work.

The whole thing felt uncomfortable to me. I felt really bad for her, and really concerned for her body. I had a long talk with her that night at the hospital. I told her that it was time to stop putting her body through all of this and that she had to start finding healthy ways of getting her emotional needs met, **now**. I told her I wasn't going to channel any more healings to her. Do I sound like a real meany? I felt like I had become one of the enablers in her life.

I'll be honest with you. I didn't know if what I was doing was right or wrong. It felt right, though. I talked to her about two months later, and she told me she was doing very well physically and that she was back in therapy herself. She said she was finding ways to get the love and nurturing she needed — other than getting sick.

When a client has made some comment about not wanting to be completely healed because they want to continue coming for healings, I tell them that their attitude has a lot to do with the healing process and that they could possibly be blocking the healing. I turn the conversation to other ways they can get nurturing, and I continue to focus on "life after illness" until they no longer come for healings.

There are better ways to get love and nurturing than being sick. Encourage your clients to find them.

Chapter 11

Cancer

I want to talk to you about **cancer**. Cancer is like the boogeyman.

As my very special friend Joan (to whom this book is dedicated) said when she found out she had cancer, "Is this the beginning of the end?" I think that's what most of us fear when we hear that a friend or a loved one has cancer.

We immediately get in touch with our sense of powerlessness over disease and death. Here's a sad thought, but one I have found to be true: at one time pneumonia killed people. So did diphtheria, smallpox, polio, malaria, the plague. I could go on and on. The point is, since medical science has found cures for these one-time dreaded diseases, we humans don't doubt God's hand in scientific cures for them — but we **do** doubt God's ability to heal the illnesses that medicine has not found a cure for. Don't you find that sad? In whom are we putting our faith, science or God?

You may be thinking, "Yeah, but so many people die from cancer. It's a horrible and devastating disease." You're right. It **can** be. I know it kills people. If our soul has chosen cancer to help us in our death process, then we are going to die. If our soul has chosen cancer for another purpose, such as a necessary spiritual transformation in this life, then we will not die. In healing, it is important to remember that we cannot make that judgment for another person. We do not know what that person's soul intends, or needs.

I remember clearly the day my friend Joan found out the county was not going to give her any help financially for a halfway house she had created for recovering alcoholic mothers. She had founded this home and kept it running for years with a combination of strength, determination and prayer. Money was always tight. She tried everything she could to keep it going, but the day she received the letter from the county denying her request for financial aid, she turned to me and said, "Echo, it looks like I have to close the house, and if I do that, I have nothing left to live for." Two months later she found out she had cancer. For two more years she tried to find something to replace the loss she felt of the halfway house, but nothing really sparked her up. She asked for very few healings during this time. I believe she knew she was in her death process.

I have seen good friends and clients go one of two ways when they find out they have cancer. They either give up, or they go all out to be healed. I think people have an inner knowledge of the process they are in, and what its purpose is in their lives.

That's where we come in as channels for healing. If a person is coming to you to get the condition called "cancer" healed, don't you try to figure out what process they are in. You just channel the energy. You don't know what your client's soul is doing. It isn't important for us to know the reason. Everything in life is a process. Your job as a channel when doing healings on someone with cancer or any disease is to focus on the healing process, **now**. Stay in the now.

I can't tell you how many times over the years I have been asked, "Can God heal cancer, too?" What an arrogant question! What we are really saying when we ask that, is: "Since medical science can't completely cure cancer, are you sure that God can?"

We **cannot**, as channels for healing, allow negativity to take over our thoughts. When visualizing the word "cancer," change the R to an L, and then you are visualizing the word "**cancel**." Cancel the negativity attached to this disease. Cancel the fears. Cancel the death thoughts. Cancel cancer!

Yes, maybe a client's soul choice will be to die, but, in the meantime, they are alive. Alive and asking for a healing. You can be instrumental in healing whatever needs to be healed.

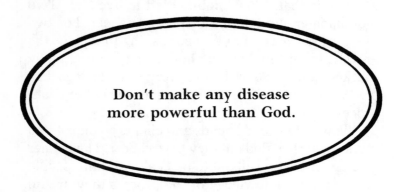

**Don't make any disease
more powerful than God.**

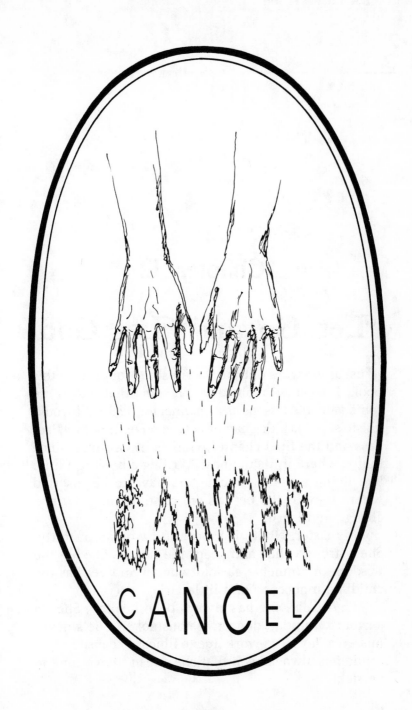

CANCEL

Chapter 12

Let Go and Let God

Just as we were putting the finishing touches on this book, I became involved in a healing that taught me some valuable lessons as a channel for healing. I would like to slip this little chapter between **Healing Is a Process** and the final chapter, **God Is in Control**, since that is where it fits the best. Writing a book is a little like living a life: new chapters have to be inserted where they fit the best as we continue to grow and change and learn.

My sister, Nikki, is a beautiful woman of thirty. She's strong-willed and keeps life simple. She has the wisdom of a ninety-year-old woman and yet has the childlike innocence of a little girl.

Physically, she has always been healthy. She's a jogger, a Tahitian dancer, a nonsmoker. She's never missed a day from work due to illness because her attitude has always been that she doesn't have time to be sick!

Six weeks ago she began having trouble breathing. Only four days passed between the time she started having problems and the day the ambulance took her to the hospital.

The X-rays showed she had a severe case of double pneumonia, so she was put in the intensive care unit. After ten days on antibiotics, she suddenly started feeling worse. They did another set of X-rays and they showed both lungs were collapsing. The doctor told us they needed to perform surgery on her to inflate the lungs and also to do a biopsy of the lung tissue. The doctor said that her blood gases indicated some kind of rare disease but that they had no idea what it was. Up to this point I hadn't done any healings on her. When we first realized she had double pneumonia, our family had called several prayer groups throughout the country. Many loving friends were praying for her recovery, and a good friend of mine, Alberto Aquas, a healer from Brazil, was sending her absentee healings every evening. I don't know why I wasn't doing any healings. I didn't feel the "urge" from inside. It felt all along like she was receiving what she needed.

Within twenty-four hours after the surgery the doctor explained to us that she did in fact have a very rare lung disease called Hamman-Rich syndrome. He said they don't know what causes it or how to cure it.

My whole family was devastated. It all seemed to happen so fast. First we all thought about her dying. It was an awful thought. All the usual thoughts ran through my mind. "It isn't fair." "Not her." "She's too young." "She's too special." "Why? Why? Why?" It didn't make sense. I felt so powerless, so helpless. What was God doing? I wanted Him to come and tell me everything was fine. I was so angry. I was scared.

We all went down to the coffee shop to have a family conference. We talked about our fears. We talked about the choices we had. Clearly we had two: we could dwell on the fifty percent who didn't recover, and allow all the negative thoughts and feelings to consume us; or, we could choose to think and feel positively. The doctor told us he was choosing to stay positive — and we decided that's the way we wanted to be, too. There was no doubt in my mind that I would start doing healings on her as soon as I saw her. I remember going into her room that night, placing my hand on her chest and asking God to please use me as an instrument in her healing process. For a second I was worried that I was too emotionally involved — but almost immediately after placing my hand on her the energy began to flow. The energy was very intense. I felt so grateful that God was working on her.

Later that night when I got home, I asked my husband to please help me remember to stay positive. I really had to discipline myself to think **only** positive thoughts. It was hard work because I had so much fear that I might have to let her go.

I have been doing healings on clients and close friends for almost twenty years, and this one has been the most difficult one to be involved with — but also the most rewarding. I have really learned some valuable lessons that I believe will make me a better channel in the future.

I understand the fears and anxieties that family members go through. I can see now why they put so much of the responsibility for their loved one's wellness on the healer. People want a "God with skin on." I understand the hopelessness and powerlessness they feel.

I went through a real tug-of-war about what to pray for. Do I pray that my sister is completely healed? Do I pray for God's will? This was difficult, because I would get fearful about what the will of God might be!

I was getting all caught up in what the "right" way to pray might be.

One night, late, I called my minister. He was sleeping, but his wife and I had a wonderful conversation. She reminded me to pray for my sister's highest good. She said possibly my sister was making a soul choice, and that I needed to work on accepting whatever that choice was.

Acceptance. Letting go. It was all so tough to do. I knew what my will for her was, so I started asking God to help **me**.

The healing energy didn't come every day. It came every other day and would last at least one hour. Slowly but progressively, Nikki was improving. When I channeled the energy, I would detach myself emotionally. I would think of her as a child of God — not as **my** sister.

Daily, I had to center myself and stay connected to God. When anyone around me would talk negatively, I had to **make** myself "rise above" the words. My minister's wife said to me, "Echo, **fatal** is a five-letter word. That is all it is. Just five letters that make up a word. You can choose whether to give that word power, or not."

Then on the days when I had given the words power and I was filled with fear, I had to talk about it, I had to cry it out. I have a responsibility to my own body not to store that negative stuff.

Instead of always projecting ahead to the outcome of Nikki's healing process, I had to stay in the "now" and be grateful for the progress we were seeing each day.

It seemed that I was learning more lessons, daily: more compassion for others, a better understanding of myself and my relationship with God. I had to remind myself daily that healing is a **process**, and no matter how strongly we want someone healed, their healing process will go exactly as it is supposed to go.

Just a few days ago the doctor told us he feels my sister is recovering from this disease, and yesterday she came home from the hospital. She needs to be on oxygen around the clock, but that may be temporary. Daily, she is healing. Daily, we are healing.

Once again I find myself telling you just how important it is to detach yourself from whomever you're channeling energy to. Socrates said:

We will not be able to cure the body until we take into consideration the soul.

Our souls are on a journey. We are on this Earth to learn and to grow. Our conscious minds are not fully aware of what we're here to accomplish, let alone understand what another person's journey entails!

Praying for someone's highest good is difficult, because it may not be what **we** feel their highest good is. But, it is certainly the most loving request we can make for someone we love.

* *

It's been five months since we wrote about my sister's condition. She is now off all medication and completely off the oxygen we all believed she'd be on forever. She is going back to work full-time.

Chapter 13

Do You Want to Dance?

I sometimes get the image of a boy-girl dance at age thirteen when I think of spiritual healers and the medical profession. We're on one side of the room — they're on the other. Everybody's afraid to make that first move. While I don't believe that is **entirely** the case anymore, many people do have the notion that spiritual healers are against the medical profession. People are surprised when I tell them not to discontinue medication while receiving healings or when I make a suggestion that they consult their doctor.

I personally believe doctors are instruments of healing too. The trouble I have is when people believe that the **only** help they have available to them for physical or emotional problems is the medical profession. People say so often that "doctors are only human," but I think there is a part of all of us that doesn't believe they are — that they are, instead, more than human. Most of us want "a god with skin on," and I think that's what we're expecting when we go to a doctor.

I have to say I haven't had a lot of experience with

the medical profession in my capacity as a spiritual healer. Most of the time when I am channeling healing to someone in a hospital, I don't talk with the doctors or nurses about what I'm doing. I have learned that it's not very acceptable. The patient sometimes gets labeled "crazy," and I have been treated with great coldness by some of the medical profession. So, instead of opening myself up to possible harassment and criticism, I just do what I'm there for, and I keep the conversation at a minimum.

I teach an eight-week, sixth sense development class which includes a class on spiritual healing. Many nurses have taken the class and are now using laying-on-hands healing with their patients. Unfortunately, they don't feel the freedom to talk about it so they do their channeling silently. In talking to one of the nurses recently, she told me she has found that when she gives her patients a back rub, the healing almost always flows from her hands without asking for it. She was telling me that she had a patient a while ago who was in a great deal of pain that the medication wasn't helping. She said the woman grabbed her arm and said, "Please do something for my pain — I know you can." So this nurse said to her, "I will channel healing to you if you don't tell anyone here that I'm doing it." She then channeled a healing to her patient for about ten minutes. The woman went right to sleep and slept for the entire night. The next day the woman asked the nurse she would "do that" again. My nurse friend said she channeled healing every night to the woman until the patient went home. Her condition had improved **greatly**.

Unfortunately, the other nurses I called to ask about their channeling didn't have such wonderful experiences to relate. The majority told me they were channeling energy — but not so that anyone knew. The

107

reason they gave was that they did not want the ridicule or, worse, they feared losing their jobs.

A few years ago a friend of mine who is a nurse went to the administration of the hospital he was working in and asked them if they would ever consider having a spiritual healer on the staff. They told him that they had a healer on staff for a time but that it made some of the patients feel insecure about the medical profession, so they let her go. They said the message the patients got was that the medical profession was admitting "We don't have all the answers." This is really unfortunate.

I called the American Medical Association recently and asked them what their position is on laying-on-hands healing and if they are aware of any medical institutions in this country that are using this type of healing. They said they have no opinion on spiritual healing and that they are not aware of any medical institutions using this work. They mentioned the book written by Dolores Krieger called *Therapeutic Touch* but made it **very clear** that "Therapeutic Touch" is **not** laying-on-hands healing (in their opinion).

I called the American Holistic Medical Association and asked them the same questions. The man on the phone told me the only place he is aware of is the A.R.E. Clinic in Phoenix, Arizona. The woman who answered the phone at the A.R.E. Clinic in Phoenix told me they use laying-on-hands healing every day in their work at the Clinic and referred me to the A.R.E. in Virginia Beach, Virginia (which is the Association of Research and Enlightenment founded by Edgar Cayce in 1927).

I called "the Beach" and spoke to a woman named Kathleen, who told me she was not familiar with any medical institutions in the U.S. other than the Clinic in Phoenix where spiritual healing is being done. She

108

referred me to Dr. Norman Shealy, M.D., Ph.D., of the Shealy Pain and Health Rehabilitation Institute in Springfield, Missouri. I wrote to Dr. Shealy and asked him if he could give me any information regarding the medical profession and laying-on-hands healing. Dr. Shealy was the first President of the American Holistic Medical Association. He is a neurosurgeon who has directed his activity toward holistic medicine since the early 1970s.

Dr. Shealy wrote me back. He told me his clinic is very interested in spiritual healing. He said, to the best of his knowledge, no real research has been done on this in the medical profession. He said there was an article in the *Journal of the American Medical Association* in 1984 on the laying-on-hands healing that came from Duneden, New Zealand, and in a survey of medical schools throughout the world they found that very few taught anything about it. Dr. Shealy also mentioned Dolores Krieger of New York University School of Nursing as being very active in promoting the concept of healing or "Therapeutic Touch" and said she has done some simple research on this.

Of the dozens of phone calls I made to find out where the medical community stands on spiritual healing, I was very surprised to find only one place, the A.R.E. Clinic in Phoenix, that openly admitted using this type of healing in their work. Some of the doctors talked about colleagues of theirs who do some "pretty far-out" things, but no one would mention any names. A couple of physicians I know personally and happen to know they channel healing energy told me **not** to mention their names in this book. The clear message I was getting over and over was: Yes, a lot of physicians are aware of spiritual healing. Yes, some of them do channel healing to their patients, **but no one wants to be recognized for it**!

In spite of the fact that **no one wants to talk about it**, I would still like to believe there are lots of doctors out there channeling the medical knowledge they have learned **and** the gift of healing they were born with. I suspect that the medical profession channels healing energy in some degree to patients without even being aware of it. They come from a scientific "let's prove and explain this" attitude, whereas we come from a spiritual "it's not necessary to prove or explain" attitude. When it comes right down to it, the important thing is that it's happening.

Several years ago I had an experience with a doctor who came for a spiritual healing. I'd like to share this story with you as it is one of my learning experiences. I pass it on to you with the hope that you don't get caught up in the same problem.

The first time he came for a healing I was very intimidated. I felt like I had to **prove** this healing method works. He didn't help my feelings of intimidation — he asked all kinds of medical questions. I felt we were talking in different languages. (We were!) He told me he did not want me to write his **real** name in my appointment book, just in case one of his patients came to me and happened to look in the book. He always wanted me to schedule enough time out so that he would be gone before my next client arrived. I gave this man a lot of power. I went along with his paranoia because I really wanted to show him that this worked. He always wanted explanations in detail of what was happening during a healing. He was getting better — but would always find a logical, rational reason for why that was so (i.e., medication he was on). It was **very** difficult for him to acknowledge the healing energy actually worked.

One day it occurred to me that we were in an "ego battle," and I was just as much at fault for what was

110

going on as he was. I had a serious talk with him about my feelings. I told him I could not explain spiritual healing in standard medical terms. I told him I was intimidated by him because he was a doctor, and that I needed to change my attitude and think of him as a person first and a doctor second. I stopped feeling so defensive about myself and what I was doing. I took my power back. Shortly after this, he stopped coming for healings.

If you find yourself in a similar situation, I caution you about giving your power away. Don't feel apologetic. Don't feel you need to prove anything. How can we explain a spiritual experience intellectually? It is not entirely possible. Something gets lost in the translation, so just leave it alone. If a client is having a difficult time understanding this, suggest to them that they pray for an understanding. They will get their answers if they do that.

I don't want you to get the impression that **all** physicians are like this man. Many are open to spiritual healing. I tell you the above so that you don't get caught up in an ego battle with someone in the medical field. Again — I really believe we're just communicating what we are doing in different languages, from different perspectives.

We are all spiritual beings. We are all channels for healing in our own way, whether we are using traditional medicine, prayer, laying-on-hands, meditation, affirmation, etc.

Just as what happens at a boy-girl dance of thirteen-year-olds, a few finally go over to the other side and say, "Do you want to dance"? Won't it be wonderful when we're all out on the dance floor with "them?" Meeting in the middle, together. No longer taking sides. When this learning and maturing does take place, we will witness a tremendous improvement in healing for all people.

Chapter 14

God Is in Control

If you're anything like I was, you still may be looking for the "secret."

For years I was sure there was a secret to laying-on-hands healing. It always seemed so mysterious. So little was written about it. Very little, if anything, was written on **how** to do a spiritual healing.

I've attended several lectures over the years on healing, always anticipating that someone would finally disclose the "mystery." Was there a special technique? A certain way to pray? A perfect way to place my hands?

Whatever you call that power greater than yourself, i.e., God, Goddess, Higher Power, Lord Almighty, Creator, Omnipotence, Universal Life Force, Infinite Spirit, Jehovah, Holy Ghost, Immanuel, Yahweh, Allah, Khuda, Brahma, Buddha or Love, that Power has a healing energy that can dissolve any physical problem created by humankind.

The healing energy is complete. It doesn't need a certain technique in order to work. God doesn't wait

115

for special prayers. The energy flows when there is a need for healing. It says in the *Bible* to ask. Jesus Christ said, ''Ask, and it shall be given unto you, according to your faith.''

The secret is: there is no secret!

God is in control as soon as you open yourself up to the energy.

I believe God loves us *unconditionally*. He wants us to be happy and healthy.

I believe that for us to accept this and want it for ourselves is what true healing is all about.

God bless and happy channeling!

Echo

NOTES

NOTES

We calculate... You delineate!

PLANETARY PROFILE: A Cosmic Road Map

A **historical breakthrough** in astrology, the *Planetary Profile* provides a unique level of **integration** and **understanding** in the interpretation of natal horoscopes.

Most computerized astrological interpretations are fragmented and choppy, discussing one factor at a time with no integration. The *Planetary Profile* searches each horoscope for **themes** and synthesizes the material.

Each *Planetary Profile* includes sections discussing:

★ identity   ★ relationships
★ work   ★ sex
★ money   ★ health
★ beliefs   ★ future trends
★ parents   ★ karmic lessons
  ★ children & creativity
  ★ mind and communication

A **special, no-charge bonus** lists all the astrolo factors which make up each theme. This *Astrolog Annotation* is a fantastic tool for honing skills at c delineation and makes a wonderful tool in astro classes. Already, some professional astrologers ordering *Planetary Profiles* in sets of two: one notated for their own use, and one without astrolo annotation to give to their clients at the end of the c sultation. You must request *Astrological Annota* if you wish it included **(free)** in any *Profile*.

The *Complete Planetary Profile* (20-30 comp pages) is available for a special, introductory pric **$18.00**. The *Concise Planetary Profile* (10-15 pa is a shortened version, focusing on the very stron themes, and is available for only **$12.00**.

ROMANCE REPORT

The *Romance Report* analyzes the relationship between two people with a focus on soulmates. Beginning with a look at each person individually, the report goes on to analyze potential interactions between the two.

A wonderful option for people interested in building a beautiful, sharing, intimate exchange with that special someone. Available for only **$8.00**.

SEER

The *Sexual Expression and Enrichment Report* analyze the sexual approach, habits, turn-ons and t offs of anyone. Written with a light touch, *SEER* help an individual keep perspective on this vital of life, allowing laughter as well as loving humorous yet caring discussion of your lovemaking style.

Pleasure and passion are at your fingertips. Send for your SEER today. Available for **$6.00**.

TUNING IN TO TRANSITS

The vast cosmic plan mirrored in the stars is revealed partly through transits. The *Interpreted Transits* provide a day-by-day preview of upcoming issues and themes.

9 planets (hard aspects only)
6 mos. **$15**___ 12 mos. **$25**___
9 planets (hard & soft aspects)
6 mos. **$18**___ 12 mos. **$30**___
Outer planets (hard aspects only)
12 mos. only **$8**___
Outer planets (hard & soft aspects)
12 mos. only **$10**___

THEMES FOR TWO

Our *Themes for Two* report considers the c of the relationship between any two people. Areas cussed include mental compatibility, communica styles, business prospects, energy levels, ideals values, security needs and potential sexual attract

This report is appropriate for business associates, parents and children, romantic involvements or any potential relationships. The text is only **$8.00** and includes the Composite Chart.

★ ★

You can order by mail or by telephone!

To order by **telephone**, use our toll-free 800 number to call between 9:00 AM and 4:00 PM, Pacific time (12-7 PM in the East, 11-6 i Midwest and 10-5 in the Mountain time zone). Ask for Astro Computing, Department HH-86 and your order will be filled immediately. Pay for that order is due when you receive your report(s) — and will include a $2.00 postage and handling charge plus a $2.00 phone cha
Our 800 number is **800 525-1786 for people calling from California** and **800 826-1085 for people calling from other states** (excepting A and Hawaii). We regret that we cannot take 800 calls from Alaska or Hawaii.
Pick up the phone or a pen and paper to get **your** personal interpretations **today**!

To order by **mail**, send the full birth data (name, day, month, year, time and place of birth) to Astro Computing Services, Dept. HH Prices and choices for each report are listed below and should be indicated on your order. If you request a report for two people, ple include the full birth data for **both** people. Enclose a check or money order for the appropriate amount — plus $2.00 for postage and hand

Options for One Person		Options for One Person	
Complete Planetary Profile ☐	Concise Planetary Profile ☐	SEER [for person #1] ☐	Transits: ⸜ hard only
For person #1 ☐ #2 ☐ **$18.00 ea.**	For person #1 ☐ #2 ☐ **$12.00 ea.**	SEER [for person #2] ☐	9 planets ☐ ⸜ hard & soft
Astrological Annotation (N/C) (Recommended for astrologers only) ☐	Astrological Annotation (N/C) (Recommended for astrologers only) ☐	**$6.00 each**	Outer planets ☐ 6 mo._ For person #1 ☐ #2 ☐ 1 year _
Asteroids also ☐ 10 Planets only ☐	Asteroids also ☐ 10 Planets only ☐	**Options for Two People** Romance Report ☐ Themes for Tw	
Indicate choice of house system. (Placidus is used if none is indicated)		(Add **$2.00** for postage and handling) **Total** ___	
If no birthtime is given, noon will be used. Astro recommends **against** ordering options other than *Transits* with an unknown birthti			

You don't need a credit card to order by phone — we trust you!

For mail orders please send check or money order (US dollars) to:

ASTRO COMPUTING SERVICES, DEPT. HH-86 • PO BOX 16430 • SAN DIEGO, CA 92116-0430
THE MOST RESPECTED NAME IN ASTROLOGY